Indians of Alabama

Guide To The Indian Tribes of The Yellowhammer State

By Scott Sewell

INTRODUCTION

By Glen Simmons

History of the U.S. Color Line

Published by Backintyme Publishing

Crofton, Kentucky, U.S.A.

Copyright @ 2016 by Backintyme

ALL RIGHTS RESERVED

Backintyme Publishing

1341 Grapevine Rd.

Crofton, KY 42217

270-985-8568

Website: http://backintyme.biz

Email:backintyme@mehrapublishing.com

Printed in the United States of America

August 2016

ISBN: 978-0-939479-47-4

Library of Congress Control Number: 2016950484

Indians of Alabama

Guide to the Indian Tribes of The Yellowhammer State

Contents

INTRODUCTION
by Glen Simmons

"Glenn, all I know is that we come from a tribe of blue eyed Indians called Black Welch". These were the words from my paternal Grandmother Sylvia Chavers Simmons to a young boy that couldn't seem to shake a consuming interest in Indians. I was a boy too young to understand how the spirit of heritage and the connectivity of ancestry can work deeply in the human soul. Black Welch, Black Dutch, Blue eyed Indians, what in the world was she thinking? So naturally I thought my Grandmother was either crazy or she was trying to throw me off the path, right? I mean who ever heard of blue eyed Indians before? At that early season of life I thought all Indians looked like the pictures I'd seen of Sitting Bull or at the very least Mingo, Daniel Boone's trusted companion. Later I would learn of a people forced to hide in plain sight behind terms like those mentioned. The only way to survive was to deny who they were.

As time passed I felt like the hope of gaining a truer perspective on my heritage grew foggier and that my ancestor's lives had become ghosts. They were fading, receding and shifting away from the light, vanishing into the land of pine and red clay from which they came. I could find no validation for my

Grandmothers words. There was an eternal missing link to who she was. The natural bridge that should remain intact between the ones you came from and who you know yourself to be was gone. She realized she only knew what little she had been told. It had been robbed from her just as it had been robbed from the generation that came before her. But in those Jim Crow years of the South it was the only way to remain safe.

Welcome to the path of many mixed blood Alabamians as well as other Southeastern Native peoples. Paths of confusion, doubt, shame, ridicule and lack of documentation have left us with only a vague sense of what elders traditionally pass down. Still, we are on a path and of a spirit that knows we are from the people that first called this continent home. We may become quiet but we never cease our searching and we will never go away.

Scott Sewell was wise enough to not just look to the past for understanding, but also to the future and the present for clarity and perspective. Of the many jewels from the present is Steve Travis, a fine historian on our culture and even finer human being.

Guide to the Indians of Alabama: The State Recognized Tribes of the Yellowhammer State is for all with ties or interests in this rich part of Yellowhammer history. It is an especially rich gift for those with native ties, helping us link from the past to the present.

Book "Introductions" are supposed to spark an interest in reading the particular book. If you are holding this book then the seed has already been planted. There is a reason it has found you and I hope in part my words lead you to read on. I think this book is an important tool for us to have. I believe your journey of understanding will be greatly aided by *Guide to the Indians of Alabama: The State Recognized Tribes of the Yellowhammer State; s*o from the Mowa Band of Choctaw, the Cherokee, Catawba, Creek and all of our brothers and sisters of mixed blood in between, I hope you will find the rich rewards that are entailed in these pages.

In its own way it is holy work, pointing to something bigger than ourselves*. Guide to the Indians of Alabama: The State Recognized Tribes of the Yellowhammer State* represents years of travel to many states, diligence, study, research and sorting all the facts from family lore. But more than any of that Scott Sewell has dedicated his journey to the love of his people, to mine and yours. It is a wonderful gift to connect us with our ancestors but maybe more importantly for those yet to come along to connect with us. The writing of this book is Scott Sewell's way of honoring his place in the sacred circle.

I travel many times each year from Nashville to my hometown of Pensacola. As I do I ride with keen awareness that I am journeying through ancient lands, Indian lands. Deep into Monroe, Conecuh and Escambia Counties where the rivers sing the songs of our ancestors. It is where the land is laden with those that came before us. This is *our* story. Aho !

Glenn Simmons
May 2016
Nashville Tennessee

AUTHORS FOREWORD

I have many familial ties to the state of Alabama and have always felt that Alabama and its unique history are one that could not get researched enough and the body of works which are more readily available today about the present realities of its Native American communities is steadily growing. The curtain of silence and isolation that was par for the course in generations gone by is today gone, replaced by a vibrant and sophisticated dialogue regarding the often complicated identity of the many Indian groups found in the Yellowhammer State.

The State of Alabama is home to thousands of people of Native American ancestry as well as many Indian tribal groups who work to maintain the balance of preserving ancient tribal identities in an increasingly complex and diverse American society. Those unfamiliar with the state may be surprised to find that there are still Native American communities alive and well in the Yellowhammer State; the American governments Indian Removal Policy of the 1830's was intended to root out all the tribal communities and "remove" them west of the Mississippi. Fortunately for the state as well as its Indian people today, this hoped for outcome was not successful. Hundreds of Indian people survived that catastrophic event as well as the many generations of poverty and social marginalization that came in its wake, with true change arriving in some communities only within living memory.

Alabama's Indian history is one of deep roots in the fertile soil, and can be traced back more than 10,000 years in the past. Reaching back to the Paleoindian Period, people have been in the region for countless generations. Over the long arc of time cultural and technological advances brought changes to the early tribal communities that inhabited what is now the state Alabama. With the passage of years, the communities of the region would transition from the Paleoindian, to the Archaic, to the Woodland, and then to the Mississippian periods; a growing sophistication would mark each step along the path of the developments of Native American societies in the area that would one day be Alabama.

While in the minds of many people today, the Mississippians culture is best known for the large and complex earthen mounds they built across the Southeast, in Alabama this civilization reached true status as a distinctive and lasting part of history most at the amazing site of the Moundville complex in Tuscaloosa County. Upon the arrival of European explorers in the area in the sixteenth century, the many distinct tribal groups known from the historic period were established and thriving in the lush bottomlands and teeming forests throughout what is now the state of Alabama.

Including such well-known tribes as the Cherokee, Choctaw, Creek, and Chickasaw, as well as the many smaller groups like the Alabamu, Koasati and Euchee, the Indians of the region were organized into complex and stratified agrarian societies pronouncedly different from the more nomadic Indians of the plains most famous to American movie-goers of a later age. With the arrival of Spanish explorers in the early sixteenth century, southeastern Indian society was subjected to continual assaults on their very survival as the spread of non-native diseases, slavery, and European incursion into tribal lands for exploitation of their resources began almost immediately after contact.

Centuries of struggle against a flood of European and later Americans into Native American lands would reach a breaking point In the 1830s, as the majority of the Native Americans in lands claimed by Alabama, as well as across the south in large part were forcibly removed from the home lands that they had resided in for millennia. The efforts by the state and federal government to remove Indians to the west of the Mississippi were to make way for cotton plantations and American dreams of expansion, to the detriment of the communities of Native

Americans. Today, The Poarch Band of Creek Indians, Echota Cherokee Tribe of Alabama, Cherokee Tribe of Northeast Alabama, Ma-Chis Lower Creek Indian Tribe of Alabama, Southeastern Mvskoke Nation, Cher-O-Creek Intra Tribal Indians, MOWA Band of Choctaw Indians, the Piqua Shawnee Tribe, the United Cherokee Ani-Yun-Wiya Nation, and many other tribal communities still maintain their identity and traditions in their tribal homelands. The nine peoples we examine in this work have recognition of a relationship between them and the state of Alabama, even as the meaning of the relationship differs among various communities.

With only a few works focused on the state tribes of Alabama and having helped in a small way with a recent work on the state tribes of South Carolina by my cousin S. Pony Hill entitled _Strangers in Their Own land: the State Recognized tribes of South Carolina_, I responded to the suggestion of Indian friends from Alabama that such a work was needed for the Yellowhammer State. Sources for information on the several groups vary greatly in their accuracy and perspective, and I utilized the Alabama Indian Affairs Commission (AIAC) website to access much of the initial information presented about the state recognized tribes of Alabama; in contact with some individuals and groups there was differing information provided about tribal history and current situations. This being said I utilized the AIAC as a primary authority for information I included in this tome, as well as Denise Bates work and interviews with members of several of the tribes discussed here.

Tribal leaders are encouraged to contact the author with any updated information and future editions will be updated. The AIAC, after an initial rocky start, is now a crucial institution working on behalf of and with the Native Americans of the region to help preserve and pass on the many diverse tribal cultures and identities found in Alabama. This state agency as it is now was in some part created by legislative action in 1984, and it represents nearly 40,000 American Indian families who are residents of the State of Alabama. The AIAC is described as being in a liaison as well as advocacy role between the various departments of the state government and the Indian people of the tribal communities. AIAC seeks to represent the Indian people of Alabama who wish to stand together with their fellow citizens, while maintaining their own cultural and ethnic heritage. The assistance of members of the commission as well as tribal; people from across the state was helpful in the compiling of this work and many thanks are due to more people than can be named herein.

The issues of identity we are examining in this work beg the thorniest of questions. Just who is an Indian? While there is no single federal, state or tribal criterion that indisputably establishes someone's identity as an Indian, the government agencies across the many levels often make use of differing criteria to decide who is an Indian in their eyes and so eligible to participate in their programs. The many tribes also have varying eligibility criteria for membership, and to gain information on each ones requirements, and to determine what the criteria might be for that particular agency or tribes, you should contact each entity directly. The information presented here is just a general guide.

When discussing Indian communities, the Bureau of Indian Affairs (BIA) is always an important part of tribal life for many tribes, especially those such as the Poarch Band of Creeks in Atmore, a tribe who are federally recognized since the mid 1980's; unlike the Poarch Band all of the others of Alabama's state recognized tribes lack acknowledgment by the BIA and the federal government. In order to be determined eligible for Bureau of Indian Affairs services, an Indian must (1) be a member of a Tribe recognized by the Federal Government, (2) one-half or more Indian blood of tribes indigenous to the United States (25 USC 479) ; or (3) must, for some purposes, be of one-fourth or more Indian ancestry. The above multiple requirements listed above in large part does exclude many people who are members of Alabama's state recognized tribes. Most of the federally originated services and programs supplied through the BIA are limited to Indians living on or near federal Indian reservations, such as Poarch.

Foundational to this small look into the Alabama tribes was a work by Denise Bates; her work <u>The Other Movement: Indian Rights and Civil Rights in the Deep South</u> (University Alabama Press; 1st Edition, released in February, 2012) was a masterful and in-depth presentation of the journey of the many now state recognized from their isolated and little known past to their oft thriving and successful modern identities. As a modern Native American with ties to the state of Alabama, I as well as many I have heard from appreciate the work she and other scholars have created over the years to give insight to the strivings of those who in times past were marginalized and dismissed.

As well information, support and encouragement from Indian friends from Alabama such as MOWA Choctaw leader Cedric Sunray; Poarch Creek genealogist Steve Travis; Wildfork Indian Community Descendent Glenn Simmons; Mekko Gordon Faye, Chris Adams, James, Cook, Justin King, and other Creek Indian members of the Kunfuskee Tallassee Tribal Town was all greatly appreciated. The dedication of these and countless other Indian people from the state of Alabama that I have been fortunate enough to befriend, to preserve the unique identity, languages, and cultures that remain is truly inspiring.

NATIVE AMERICANS IN ALABAMA

ANCIENT ROOTS

The land that is today the state of Alabama has been the home of countless communities for possibly ten thousand years or more, beginning with the Paleo-Indian peoples who the archaeological records show were living in the area at least that far back. Humanity has shaped and been shaped by the land of today's Alabama for countless generations on end. Few states can be said to be molded linguistically in its place names as much as Alabama. The name of the state itself, like tens of thousands of its citizens has Native American roots. The naming of the Alabama River by early European-Americans and subsequently of the entire state comes from the Alabama people, a Muskogean-speaking people of the Creek Nation who lived below the confluence of the Coosa and Tallapoosa rivers on the upper reaches of the river in former times.

Today the Alabama people who gave the state its name live for the most part in communities in Oklahoma and Texas. According to some sources, in the Alabama tribal language, the term for an Alabama person is Albaamo, Albaama or Albàamo

1

dependent on dialect and speaker, with the plural form being Albaamaha (Sylestine, Hardy, & and Montler, 1993). While the spelling of the word varies greatly among historic archival sources, the earliest use of it appears in several accounts of the Spaniard Hernando de Soto's expedition of 1540, with Garcilaso de la Vega using Alibamo, while the Knight of Elvas and Rodrigo Ranjel wrote Alibamu and Limamu, respectively, in attempts to transliterate the term.

The Spanish were not the only early adopters of the European use of the name; in records from 1702, the French called the tribe the Alibamon. French maps from the era identify the river as Rivière des Alibamons. Historic sources are unclear as to the exact meaning of the word, with the sources having sometime conflicting accounts. The Jacksonville Republican proposed that it meant "Here We Rest" in an 1842 article, and the usage of this translation became popular in the 1850s via the writings of Alexander Beaufort Meek.

Despite the popularity of this purported translation of the word, linguistic experts in the Muskogean languages could not find any evidence from research into the term to support such a translation. Some scholars posit that the word comes from the Choctaw word alba, meaning "plants" and amo which translate as "to gather"). There were times long before the Creek, Cherokee, or Choctaw lived here when this same land was known by other peoples by other names, most never to be known. For many thousands of years people have called the rich lands of the region home. The Alibamu people who originated in the state's name no longer can be found in its borders, today living predominately on the Alabama-Coushatta Indian Reservation in Livingston, TX and in several groups in Oklahoma.

Pre-European settlement of the rich bottomlands and lush forests of the region was extensive, with Indian peoples of many diverse languages and cultures lived in the area that is now Alabama for countless thousands of years before European colonization began. Then roots of human occupation are deep in the Alabama soil; In Russell Cave in Jackson County charcoal from ancient camp fires in the cave has been dated as early as 6550 to 6145 BC. Waterways were always highways of the ancient world and intertribal trade routes existed with the northeastern tribes, with goods moving via the many rivers to countless far away locations. Interactions with communities on the Ohio River began during the Burial Mound Period extending from 1000 BC to BCE 700 and continued until the first European contact ("Alabama", 2006).

The Moundville Archaeological Site in Hale County Alabama was occupied by peoples of the Mississippian culture from 1000 to 1450 AD. Mississippian culture was primarily agrarian and covered most of the region of modern Alabama from 1000 to 1600 AD. After Cahokia in present-day Illinois, the epicenter of the Mississippian Culture, One other of its major population centers were constructed at what is today the Moundville Archaeological Site in Moundville, Alabama, the second-largest complex of the classic Middle Mississippian era. Among the historical tribes of Native American people living in the area of present-day Alabama were several distinct yet related cultures.

THE HISTORIC ERA

Living in the area of the modern state of Alabama at the time of first European contact were many tribes, including the Cherokees, an Iroquoian-speaking people, the Muskogean-speaking Alabama, Chickasaw, Choctaw, Creek, and Koasati among the largest groups. Though part of the same large family of Native American languages, the Muskogee tribes had each developed distinct cultures and languages over the centuries of their occupation of lands in the south. While Alabama is today a diverse place with many different races, languages, and identities, the path from the days of first contact with Europeans and the enslaved Africans they brought with them through until today has been at times painful and violent. In its earliest years, planters and traders from the Upper South came to the rich lands of the Indian tribes to seek their fortune.

Many of these early wealthy settlers brought slaves with them. The population of the Alabama territory would expand exponentially as the cotton plantations and the economy in the region expanded and the settlers cast hungry eyes on the vast lands of the Cherokee, Creek, Choctaw, and Chickasaw Nations. With time the economy of the entire South was to be built primarily around large cotton plantations whose White owners' wealth grew annually, largely from slave labor. These wealthy planters and their slaves were not despite years of depictions on popular movies and books depictions of the "Old South" the only settlers in the area by far. The territory also drew countless poor and disfranchised people seeking better fortunes, many who became subsistence farmers. The fact is that the vast majority of White southerners who came to live in Alabama would never own a slave and would work nearly as hard to survive, especially after the devastation of the Civil War.

The Indians of Alabama

Alabama had a population estimated at fewer than 10,000 people in earliest decade of the 1800's, but it had expanded to more than 300,000 people by the turn of 1830. This decade was an important one in the lives of Native Americans of the region as much of the Native American population were forcibly removed from Alabama within a few short years of the passage of the Indian Removal Act by Congress in 1830, though not without determined resistance by many tribes. Thankfully, as history would show the erasing of the American Indian from the land of Alabama was not successful, though the years after the Indian removals of the 1930's until our own time were trying and difficult ones for all the Indian people who remained, few in number and impoverished for the most part. Some experts place the numbers of Native Americans who remained not enslaved and in Alabama after the removals as low as a few hundred souls all told.

Native American persons even today are still less than one percent of the states growing population of 4,779,736 according to the 2010 Census, and the 20th Century was one of the most trying times to be Native American in the state. Indian lives were difficult as the specter of Jim Crow segregation during the first half of the century kept many of Indian ancestry in the shadows, fearing discrimination and being cast to the social fringe as happened to many who were unable to avoid the county and state authorities' efforts at times to label them as "colored, mulatto, and negro".

Some things would change during the second half of the 1900's as people who were returning from war and travel in a wider world would begin the process of social change, one that in some ways continues to happen. During the mid-twentieth century especially, a movement began in which Native American communities within Alabama increasingly began demanding recognition as a group and seeking an end to discrimination against them. The social and legal history and ethnic identity of many of the groups dwelling in Alabama since the removal in the 1830's was for some authorities problematic. Due to the long history of slavery and Jim Crow racial segregation, the states self-identified Native Americans, many who were not of solely American Indian ancestry but were of mixed race, had insisted on having their cultural identification respected as a wave of change regarding race and justice swept across the American society from sea to sea.

In the decades before the end of segregation, the self-identification by many Indians was often overlooked or even subverted as the Alabama state and local authorities tried to impose a binary view of racial identity, seeking to breakdown all of society into white or black. With the successes by African Americans in demanding justice for the wrongs of the past and present Native American leaders emerged who would fight for Native American people in the state. Several communities across the state would seek acknowledgement for their claims to tribal identity and pursue petitions to the federal government for tribal recognition as sovereign nation. Only one Alabama tribe would succeed in gaining federal acknowledgment ultimately but the effort led to many changes for Indian people in Alabama as well as the creation of state recognition for tribes and the AIAC.

The roots of the several state groups emerged early in America's history in some cases, as is seen in the work of William Harlen Gilbert Jr. who issued a report to the Smithsonian Institute in 1948 asserting that southern Indians were on the way to extinction; he would have been stunned to discover that twenty years later these same groups compromised the largest percentage of petitioners for both state and federal recognition in the nation. For countless tribal groups in the south as with many elsewhere, having to produce documentation to prove their Indian identities after years of marginalization is one of the biggest ironies of their story. The appearance of widespread inter-tribal efforts, led by charismatic leaders to consolidate the isolated interests of diverse Indian groups would be challenged by Alabama's state acknowledged groups varied appearances, cultural traditions and the public's acceptance of their asserted Indian identities.

While some groups tried mightily, they would fail to garner federal recognition because some authorities asserted that the modern tribes descended from racial amalgamations that they said made it impossible to discern undiluted Indian identities. The clutching hands of Jim Crow were not easily shaken off even after the end of segregation as perceptions of the racial identity of people as black or white lingered long after "whites only" signs were taken down across the south. In part emerging from the isolation of the past into a new world of possibilities, it was a shared experience of the cold war era Indian policies and the experience of native American soldiers returning from WWII that opened a new perspective; the insights and travels of the military service created a way for Indians to see themselves as a nationally unified group and to step forward seeking sovereignty, social justice, and the preservation of their unique tribal identities and cultures.

Across the Jim Crow South, Native Americans were in many cases barred admission to White schools and often avoided admission to Black schools. Many didn't get access to any educational opportunities while a few were able to gain entrance to special "Indian schools", which were often "small, poorly equipped, poorly taught, and poorly attended".

The overarching binary orientation to race used by the south denied not only the miscegenation of the past but the actual multiracial reality of the present era. Dr. Anthony Parades, a leading researcher and Advocate for the Poarch Creeks said that during the civil rights struggle "new fault lines became evident in the racial system of the south (as) many Indians sought even more distance between themselves and any identification with blacks." Indians from Alabama began to seek better lives, and to speak up for their share of the American dream in greater numbers across the south and state of Alabama; The 1961 American Indian Chicago Conference was attended by Calvin McGhee and other leaders from Alabama and Florida's panhandle seeking to empower Indians in Alabama.

Getting the Indians to emerge from social isolation and get involved in the movement towards tribal recognition was difficult. As Eddie Tullis said once when interviewed on the political actions he remembered from his youth, "no tribal operations that went on until about, 'til I was well up in my teens, 'til about 1948 I think was the first time that there was really organized activity amongst our people". A similar statement could be applied to most of the tribes in Alabama during the first half of the 20th century.

The long arc of history would see the scattered fragments that survived the Indian removals of the 1830's turn inwards and survive a century of racial oppression only to blossom in the late 1900s into a thriving and renewed community of diverse and unique tribal peoples, bound by a common past and hopeful future today.

TODAY

The path to resurfacing into the mainstream of Alabama and American society has not been easy for most of the tribal groups of the state; the struggle to implement formal governments and seek recognition from their peers often seeming like one step forward and two steps back at first. Overcoming internal and external biases about the meaning of "Indian-ness", breaking through institutional gridlock, navigating often preferential political pitfalls, surmounting frequent and continual fiscal challenges and finding ways to mitigate the assimilative effects of modernity on the tribal peoples across Alabama being a task not easily accomplished. The very existence of tribes that remain is amazing, as Justin King, a Poarch Creek and public school teacher said "We are lucky to be here at all with everything the South has thrown at us the last two hundred years!" The same could be said of almost all the tribes in the state.

Initial efforts in the mid twentieth century to organize the Native American communities of the state had mixed results, with several setbacks and difficulties across the decades. Ultimately by the advent of the Davis-Strong Act legislation of 1984, the state of Alabama in cooperation with Native American communities and advocacy activists in the state established the Alabama Indian Affairs Commission, an organization which was slated by the legislature to acknowledge and represent the Native American citizens in the Yellowhammer state. This accomplishment occurred after long years of struggle by many people and communities, a movement to give a forum to Native Americans of the state in which they could communicate, network, and advocate for their positions as unique communities. At the time of its implementation, it recognized seven tribes that did not have federal acknowledged status.

The commission members, representatives of the tribes, have created rules for tribal recognition, which were last updated in 2003, under which several more tribes have been recognized. The Alabama state government has been active in supporting its Native citizens in efforts to preserve and celebrate Alabama's

Native American heritage, and has promoted recognition of Native American contributions to the state. With the designation in 2000 for Columbus Day to be jointly celebrated as American Indian Heritage Day, Alabama again showed its support for its Indian citizens and the states heritage. The Native American heritage is indeed and important part of the "DNA" of the state of Alabama and the southern states in general. Citizens of this region often have higher rates of Native American ancestry than their counterparts from the north, and hundreds of years of intermixture by all the races in the region have created a genetic patchwork quilt that is unique and diverse.

Despite Alabama's perception as a place with a history of intolerance and bigotry, a view that has been forwarded for years by filmmakers and media accounts, the reality is of a place with a multilayered and complex heritage that today is celebrating a rich and vibrant modern identity. The future of the state and its Native American peoples is one that is promising and full of potential. Works covering the Indians of the south were sparse, with one compiled in 1979, another in 1992, and an additional one in 2001 providing the main body of literature on Native Americans in the south in the post-civil rights south.

The Poarch Creek was "permitted" to remain in the south during the removal of the other large southern tribes, it was only to be forgotten and abandoned by the federal authorities, and ultimately the community came to be perceived as "objects of suspicion, prejudice, and discrimination by certain elements of white society." From the founding of their Homecoming Powwow in 1971, the Poarch Creeks have been leaders among Alabama's Indians in the assertion of their rights as a sovereign government. Wendell Mitchell an Alabama state senator sponsored a bill in 1976 that created the first Alabama Creek Indian Council, the earliest attempt to create a liaison between the tribes and the state government. This was followed by the Mims Act in 1978 which made changes to the evolving relationship, and would ultimately arrive at current legislation and Alabama Indian Affairs Commission, not without significant struggle though.

With the growth in understanding by groups across the state of the processes leading to recognition and increased access to services, tribes crossed the threshold to more formal political organizational efforts; the United Cherokee tribes officially organized in 1978, the MOWA Choctaw in 1979, the Jackson County Cherokee in 1981 and the Cherokee of SE Alabama in 1982, but all found that during this era the Poach creeks interests were at the forefront of tribal-state relations, a situation that would remain so for years to come, and one that was difficult for other groups to reconcile. The leadership that was exhibited by Poarch creek leaders such as Eddie Tullis, who led the Poarch Band of Creek Indians through the federal acknowledgment process and established them more as a tribal nation and less so as "an underrepresented fringe group hidden away" as one scholar put it was crucial in their successful bid for recognition by the federal government.

The tribes in some cases inspired as well as competed with one another in moving forward with their vision for a brighter future. Step by step they moved towards a restoration of their dignity as communities with north Alabama's "Jackson County Cherokee" changed their name to the Cherokee Tribe of Northeast Alabama in 1983, having organized initially in 1981. Similarly the United Cherokee Tribe of Alabama first organized in Daleville in 1978, with the Echota Cherokee emerging from it in 1980, headquartered in Shelby County. The Cherokees of Southeast Alabama organized in in Houston County in 1982.The Star Clan of Muscogee organized in Pike County in 1975, initially called the Eufaula Star Clan., and were active in economic development early on, gaining access to federal grants for Indian education monies as early as 1972. In 1985 the MaChis Lower Creeks in Coffee County developed under the guidelines of the

AIAC and became the forest tribe in Alabama to organize under the new criteria set up by the AIAC. Somewhat later, on July 10, 2001 the Alabama Indian Affairs Commission recognized the Piqua Sept of Ohio Shawnee Tribe as an Indian tribe in the state of Alabama, thus making the Piqua Sept the first petitioning group to be recognized in 17 years.

The success of some of the tribes in Alabama in garnering recognition of the state brought the ire of some federal recognized tribes who felt that many were undeserving of such; Cherokee nation's first female Principal Chief Mankiller sent a letter to the governor of Alabama, Guy Hunt stating that although many state governments in the United States had "incidental dealings" with some Indian tribes through the years, it was well established that federal law and the federal governments constitutionally mandated relationship with Indian tribes was the "sole authority to deal with and regulate American Indian tribes". That state is indeed what many of the groups striving for state recognition had in many cases as their ultimate goal.

With much smoke but little fire in the initial years of struggle to implement funding and programs for newly recognized state tribes, the going effort to capture attention for their needs slowly gained traction. In the early years the Indian tribes invested more in the state Indian Commission than did the state itself in the view of many. Tribal leaders from across the state worked during the earliest years of the state tribe's efforts to create a meaningful relationship with the state Indian Affairs commission, only to be repeatedly ignored or rejected. Lindy Martin of the Jackson County Cherokee, Diane Weston of the Echota Cherokee, Tom Davenport of the Star Clan of Muscogee, and Galasneed Weaver of MOWA were among such leaders who were initially kept at arm's length in their efforts to become part of the Alabama Indian Affairs Commission in the 1980's. As one leader said of their aims, "Anything other than equality is intolerable."

Concerns about the legitimacy of some of the groups seeking state recognition played a role in the difficult path the Indian Affairs Commission had to establishment, since as Eddie Tullis said "We have to accept the fact that there are some people who want to be Indians that are not Indians...", and this perspective led him and other leaders to at times have a very rocky relationship with other groups in the state, communities that Tullis felt could lead to Alabama becoming known nationally as the home to "fake Indians". Such sentiments would cause a distancing between the leadership of some of the groups, such as the MOWA, and the Indian Affairs Commission at times.

The Indians of Alabama

The road to today's Alabama Indian Affairs Commission has been a rocky one at times over the last 40 odd years as the states 'first people' have emerged from the social marginalization some lived in. The Davis-Strong Act that was legislated in 1984 would allow for the ultimate creation of a body that in time would include the tribes who are sate recognized to day in Alabama, though the path to it had many episodes of stop and go before the Davis-Strong act. Remarkably, the Poarch Band of Creeks would become federally recognized that same year, and would move into "deeper waters" politically speaking, taking advantage of the many benefits that the government to government relationship provides and surging forward with many projects relating to economic development, tribal housing, and the like on their newly established reservation near Atmore.

Forward momentum that sought to redress systematic blocks to Alabama Indians assertions of their identity fell slowly but steadily, such as when the attorney general of Alabama Don Siegelman allowed for the states Native Americans to identify themselves as "Indians" if they were enrolled with one of the state tribes. Across the spectrum the lives of Alabama's Indian people improved greatly, and a part of the south where people were once tightly bound by a biracial view of identity was home to a rebirth of the Indian identity on a large scale, and one which many would say continues. The development of formal tribal governments by Indian groups in the decades past was important steps in an ongoing process. It was their vocal assertions and attempts to grasp political authority and bring about local level changes that can be viewed as having been a profitable investment for today's vibrant and active Indian communities across the state.

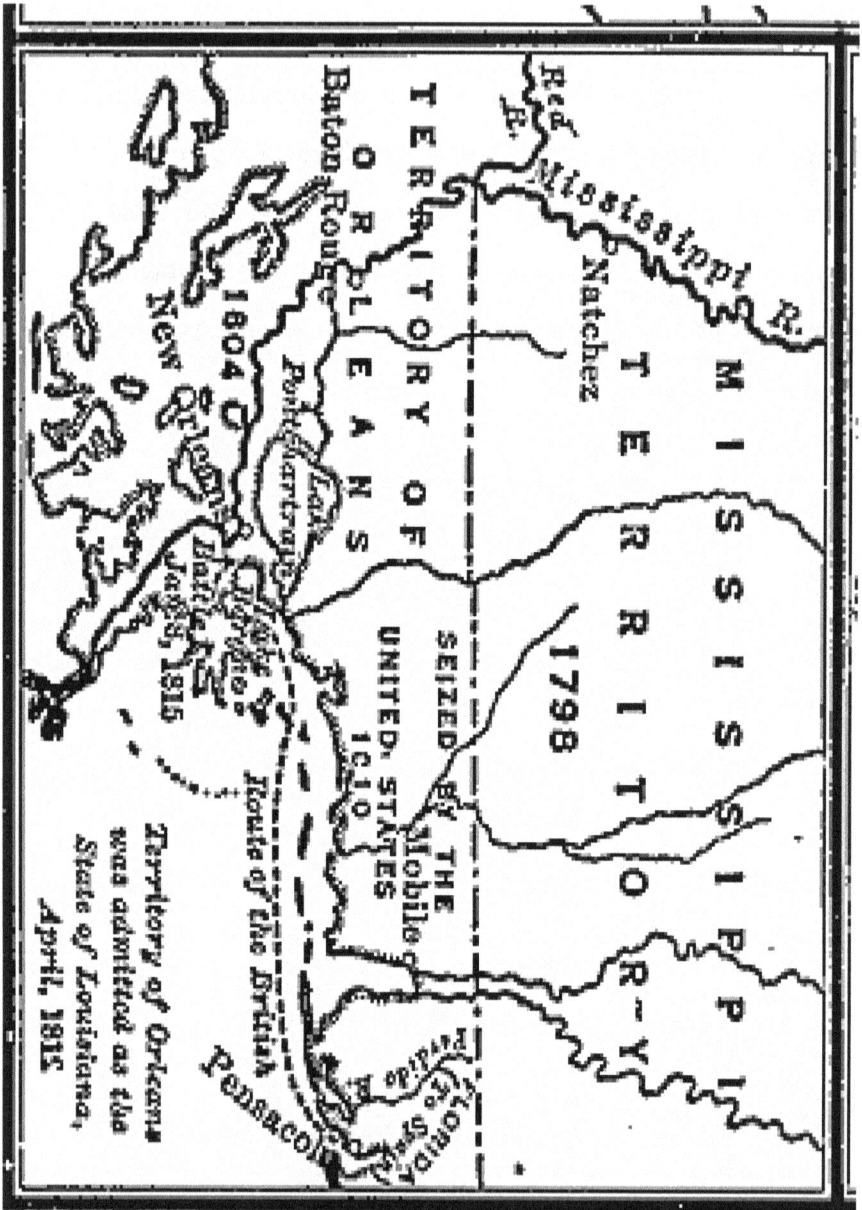

Map Mississippi Territorial 1798

ALABAMA PLACE NAMES WITH NATIVE AMERICAN ORIGINS

There are few states with as many place names having Native American origins as is found in Alabama, these many names speaking to the depth that the Native American people are part of the fabric of the state's identity. Once home to several of the most powerful tribes of the south, including the Choctaw, Chickasaw, Creek, and Cherokee, the heritage and impact of these tribe's millennia of occupation later cut short by the Indian Removal Act are still found in the hundreds of places which still bear their languages to describe. Many times the original Indian words are changed and become different from the Native American pronunciation, sometimes transformed beyond recognition of the original term.

In reconstructing a words journey from one language to another it is sometimes impossible to know its original meaning or pronunciation, and the list offered here is but a small attempt to touch on some of the most well-known of the many words from the tribal past of the region that still live on in the many place names found across the state. The short list below is just some of these words that the Choctaw, Creek, and Cherokee all lent words to today's map of the communities and geographical features of the state.

Alabama and Alabama River - named for the Alibamu, a tribe whose name derives from a Choctaw phrase meaning "plant-cutters", it became the name of the state and one of its major waterways

Autauga County - named for the Alibamu town of Atagi, the Alabamu were one of the largest ethnicities in the Creek Nation, many of whom are still found in Oklahoma and Texas

Arbacoochee – rooted in the Muskogean word "abihkuchi", translated as "a pile (as ashes) at the base", the Arbeka tribal town was an important community of the Creeks in historic times

Attalla - from the Cherokee word otali, meaning "mountain"

Bashi - adaptation of the Choctaw word bachaya , meaning a line, row, or course

Bogue Chitto - from a Choctaw word for a creek or stream and chito, meaning big

Boligee - originally a war name, it possibly originates from the Choctaw words booli (to strike) and tusha (to cut to pieces)

Buttahatchee River - from the Choctaw, bati meaning "sumac", and hahcha the Choctaw word for a river or watercourse

Cahaba- most likely derives from a corruption of two Choctaw words, oka (water) and uba "above"

Chattahoochee River - from the Muskogean words cha-to meaning "rock" and huchi (marked), and relates to the sometimes practice of Creek villages along waterways having a large painted rock to mark the landing where canoes would arrive

Chattooga River - from the Cherokee, jitaaga "chicken" or from the Muskogee (Creek) word cato (rock); there are many words such as this with disputed translations

Cheaha Mountain – taken from the Choctaw word chaha (high)

Chewacla and Chewacla State Park – both purportedly originate from the Hitchiti word sawackla; sawi meaning "racoon" and ukli meaning "town"; the Hitchiti language was one of several "minority languages spoken in the Creek Nation, as were Alibamu and Euchee

Chickasaw – rendered often for the Chickasaw tribe once present in the western part of the state, today the majority of the tribe live in Eastern Oklahoma

Choctaw County – like the above, it is named in honor of the Choctaw tribe, once resident of the region on a wide scale before removal, today they reside in Oklahoma and other parts of the south

Choctawhatchee River – derived from the Choctaw word hacha (river) and the name of the Choctaw tribe, once one of the largest tribes in the region

Conecuh County and Conecuh River - probably from the Muskogee (Creek) terms, koha (canebrake) and anaka (to be nearby), these are found in the heart of what was once the "Old Creek Nation"

Coosa County and Coosa River- origin could be the Choctaw word koshak (cane)

Coosada - after the Coushatta tribe purportedly, they were one of the many tribal towns of the Creeks

Cusseta – named after a Muscogee (Creek) tribal community prominent among the Lower Creeks

Eastaboga- from Muskogee, este (person), the indicator term ak (in water, a low place), and pokv (being dead) and most likely relates to a historic event

Escambia County - from the Choctaw words oski ambeha (possibly meaning cane therein), this area is rich in Native American and colonial history

Escatawpa- "escatawpa" signified a creek where cane was cut, with uski meaning "cane", a meaning "there", and tapa meaning "cut" in the Choctaw language; River cane were an important resource to all Indians of the south

Etowah - possibly from a Cherokee settlement of the same name which played a major role in the history of the Cherokee Nation, its meaning is unclear

Eufaula - from the Muscogee (Creek) tribal town, one which has many descendents in the state still

Eutaw - possibly from the Cherokee term, iitaawaa (long leafed pine tree), a species found across the region

Kahatchie- from the Muskogee (Creek) words koha (cane) and hache (creek), this plant was once common along most waterways and was utilized multiple ways as an important part of the Native American culture across the ages

Letohatchee - from the Muskogee (Creek) li ito fachita, possibly meaning those who make arrows straight

Loachapoka - from the Muskogee (Creek) meaning loca poga (turtle killing place), a tribal town of the Creeks, many of whom live in the area of greater metro Tulsa Oklahoma today

Lubbub- from the Choctaw word lahba, meaning "warm"

Luxapallila- from Choctaw luksi a balali, possibly meaning "turtles crawl there"

Mobile- named for a group of the Alibamu, from Spanish Mauvila, possibly from Choctaw moeli, meaning to row, or paddle; there existed a pidgin "trade jargon" by the same name during the colonial era that was used by all as a common tongue for interactions

Nanafalia - from the Choctaw, nanih meaning a hill and falaiya (long)

Notasulga - from the Muskogee (Creek) words noti sulgi (many teeth)

Noxubee- from the Choctaw word nakshobi (to stink)

Oakmulgee – originating from the Hitchiti word ockmulgee, meaning "bubbling water", once atribal town of the Creeks, today a community of the same name is the tribal capital of the modern Muscogee (Creek) Nation in Oklahoma

Ohatchee - possibly comes from the Muskogee (Creek) terms oh hacci (upper stream)

Oneonta - from the Iroquoian oneyota, possibly meaning "protruding stone"

Opelika - from the Muskogee (Creek) words opilwa lako, meaning big swamp

Panola - from Choctaw word ponola, meaning cotton, something long associated with the region

Pintlala - from the Muskogee (Creek) word pithlo, a "canoe", and the verb form of halata, "to drag"

Sepulga River – thought to originate from the Muskogee (Creek) name of svwokle, a tribal town of the Creek Nation

Sipsey River – coming from the Choctaw word sipsi (cottonwood)

Talladega, Talladega County, and Talladega Springs - Talladega is derived from the Muskogee (Creek) words italwa (tribal town), and atigi (at the end, on the border)

Tallahatta Springs - adapted from the Choctaw words, tali (rock) and hata (white)

Tallapoosa County and Tallapoosa River –locations originating from the Choctaw words tali (rock) and pushi (to pulverize), and one of several groups of related tribal towns

Tallassee - from the Muskogee (Creek) words talwa hasi (old town), and one of several groups of related tribal towns

Tensaw and Tensaw River - Etymology is unknown, possibly from a Natchez tribal term, it was a place ancestral to the Poarch Band of Creek Indians of today

Tibbie – possibly a shortened form of the Choctaw word "oakibbeha", meaning "blocks of ice are there" according to some

Tombigbee River - from the Choctaw, Itte-ombee-eye ika-abee "wooden box-making river"

Tuscaloosa and Tuscaloosa County - derived from Muskogean words "tas-ki" meaning warrior and loosa (black)[1].

Tuscumbia – originates from the Choctaw warname of tashka (warrior) and abi (killer)

Tuskegee - from the Koasati word tasquiqui, meaning warriors, as well as being a tribal town of the Creeks

Uchee- named for Uchee Creek, which in turn, was named for the Yuchi tribe, a non-Muskogee speaking constituent of the Creek Nation[2].

 Waxahatchee Creek - from the Muskogee (Creek) wakse (a clan name) and hache (stream)

Wetumpka - from the Muskogee (Creek) words "wewa tumka", or rumbling water, and one of several groups of related tribal towns.

---

[1] Chief Tuscaloosa is known to history for his courageous leading of a battle against Spanish conquistador Hernando de Soto as he passed through tribal lands in 1540. The Black Warrior River, originally named Tuskaloosa River, is also named in his honor.
[2] "yuchi" probably means "at a distance" in the Yuchi language, with yu meaning "at a distance" and chi meaning "sitting down".[45]

ASPECTS OF ALABAMA INDIAN CULTURES

STOMP DANCE

One of the most ancient cultural traditions once common to almost all tribes of the region was the Stomp Dance, and though much less well known than the modern Native American Powwow, it is again growing in popularity and participants across the state, especially as tribal groups work to restore ties to their own tribally specific cultural traditions. The Stomp Dance of the Southeastern Indians is in some ways not only a form of dance but is also an event in itself. The Stomp Dance, most often as a part of the ancient Green Corn Dance tradition though not always still is practiced by many of the Native peoples of the southeastern United States from Florida to Oklahoma. A stomp dance is usually a nighttime event, though there will be other different and specifically named dances performed as well for example the Friendship Dance, the Old People Dance or the Crawfish Dance. At the heart of the event though lies the most common of the southern Indians dance forms, simply known as the Stomp Dance.

Of the modern groups of Native Americans who have some historical ties to the state, the stomp dance is performed in large part by the Creek, Cherokee, and Yuchi peoples now located in Oklahoma, but in many ways these are similar to those found in Alabama prior to the Indian Removal Policy and subsequent banishment of many of these tribes to the west of the Mississippi in the 1830s. The style of dance though is not only restricted to tribes once of the deep south; Eastern Woodlands tribes, including the Caddo, Shawnee, Delaware, and Chickasaw, perform the Stomp Dance as well in their tribal traditions.

Stomp dances are the central activity in many Indian communities and are performed several times a year during the summer months at the tribal town or ceremonial grounds. These events are linked to natural cycles of the seasons and agriculture and are timed according to a ritual calendar. The keeping of this ancient pattern is in many ways specific to each distinct community and its ceremonial ground's established protocols.

These ceremonial Squares or "Stomp Grounds" as they are sometimes called are not only places but are also social organizations. They are both social and religious in nature; membership is not automatic but is participatory, much like houses of worship or fraternal orders in mainstream American culture. The square ground as the place of the meeting sometimes referred to, is the physical location where stomp dances take place. A ceremonial ground person's membership in the tribal town is often determined by participation, family relationships, sometimes through descent and marriage and the community of a square ground is often time called the "tribal town".

Typical architecture of a ceremonial ground is an area squared on each side by arbors, and a round dance area where the sacred fire is located during ceremonial times. The brush covered clan arbors that surround the dance area and provide seating for the ground's male members are situated within a larger ring that includes the ground's stickball field and pole. Somewhat open camps where families' camp out during ceremonial occasions are located on the periphery of the dance grounds and it is here where food is prepared and served to members and guest alike. In a long line of spiritual architecture, the spatial dimensions and layout of today's Indian ceremonial ground is similar to those in ancient tribal towns of millennia ago. This isn't by accident as many ceremonial grounds in Oklahoma and even one in Alabama can trace their origins to the tribal towns once found throughout the Southeast before the Indian removal wiped them away.

Evening stomp-dance and other ceremonies' are often part of the annually held Green Corn Ceremony, as well as taking place at other times of the year as well.

Gordon Fay, Lojah Harjo

"The Stomp Dance is at the heart of our Southeastern Indian Culture" said one 75 year old elder from Kunfuskee Tallassee grounds, Mekko Gordon Fay, known in his Creek language as Lojah Harjo "it is a time of fellowship with each other and the Creator, and is a powerful medicine for creating a balanced and healthy life in the old Indian way. Even though it is thousands of years old for those who maintain it is still a source of strength and understanding". Following the protocols of generations of ceremonial participation by the people, the stomp dancing continues throughout the night with participants staying awake until the next day.

The restrictions and sacrifices made by participants are by some viewed as an obligation that guarantees the community's wellbeing for the next year. "With these ways of our elders, we can maintain a healthy and happy life, as the Almighty, our Creator intended for us all" as Muscogee Creek elder Sam Procter put it, who still leads stomp dances across the country in Creek communities though he is in his 80's. "These ways are good for us" he adds with a smile. For almost forty years, he and other Oklahoma Creeks have come annually to the Poarch Creek Indian Reservation near Atmore, Alabama to share in the celebration of the ancient traditions of the southeastern tribes, such as Stomp Dance and Stickball games. He was instrumental in returning "Sacred Ashes" to the southern Indians and restoring the old ways to the Creeks there. Elders such as Sam Proctor, Dave Lewis, and Gordon Fay worked ceaselessly to bring the traditional

"Stomp Ground" ways of the southern Indians back to its original homeland.

Sam Proctor, medicine maker (Hillis haya) of Wakokiye Tallassee Ceremonial Grounds, Creek Nation. His son Ruben took over his place in 2015, due to health reasons.

During any Stomp Dance a man is chosen by the dance ushers, called stickmen by some, to lead the singing for another round of dancing, consisting of several episodes of differing songs he will sing one after another, unique to him as a leader. The dancers will break up after him and a new leader chosen for the next round. A Stomp Dance leader may be chosen for his singing skills or to recognize the visiting ceremonial ground he represents amongst the several present to help.

When the next stomp leader is announced the people file into the ceremonial square and begin circling its sacred fire, as others wishing to participate in the dance hurriedly line up behind the leader in a single file line which spirals counter-clockwise around the fire, man followed by woman in a pattern as old as the mounds. The leader and other dancers move forward throughout the dance, alternately walking and dancing, using a stomping step that is taken in time with the singing and shaking of the turtle or cans worn on the calves by the women. It is from the "stomping step" of the dance which it takes its English name from, and its spiral formation and rising and falling sound are like a swirling storm of people, patchwork, and Stetson hats sporting white Crane feathers; this slowly whirling hurricane of heartfelt fellowship is an ancient connection to countless generations of southeastern Indian ancestors.

A man followed by a woman, then another man followed by a woman, together the dancers alternate one after another in position behind the lead singer of the dance. Small children, at the end of the line run to keep up with the swirling group of dancers, laughing and singing intermingling with the din of the dancers movements. Across the night air the call-and-response songs of the leader and the answering shouts of the people floats. Time is kept by the shell shakers, and the women establish a correct rhythm timed with the singer's performance, setting the pace by shaking their treasured sets of leg rattles made from turtle shells or empty milk cans that the Stomp Dance women wear around their calves.

Woven by hand, chevron decorated finger-woven yarn "stomp dance sashes" are worn by many of the attendees, as well as beautiful and colorful patchwork skirts and vests. Stomp Dances in many cases can go on all night, the fellowship continues until the sun rises, and the event is concluded until the next time. At the Hassossa Tallassee Ceremonial Ground on the Poarch Creek Indian Reservation near Atmore, Alabama this ancient tradition of the Stomp Dance continues to be carried at this small Indian communities traditional Creek gatherings, often times visited by other stomp dancers from as far away as Oklahoma, Texas, Louisiana and Florida.

POWWOW

Powwow is one of the most widespread and well known aspects of modern Native American culture, and there are hundreds held across Alabama annually by most of its Indian tribes as well as other organizations. Pow Wows are the way people of the Indian community most often meeting together. Indians and visitors alike join in dancing, singing, visiting, renewing old friendships, and often make new ones in the environment of fellowship and fun found at most Powwows. This is a time for people to renew Native American cultural ties and preserve the rich heritage of American Indians as a warrior people with a distinct history. In the current world of Powwow culture, several people from Alabama have made their mark, including Chris "Dingding" Blackburn, Alex Alvarez, and others.

Powwow songs and their singers are very important in the Native American culture. Powwow songs are of many types varieties, from honoring to War Dance to socials. The Medicine Tail Singers, a "Northern-style" drum group and Native American Performance troupe from the Poarch Indian Community are one of many fine drum groups from Alabama. When Indian tribes gathered together, they share their songs, sometimes changing the songs used so singers of different tribes could take part.

Because of these changes came the use of vocables to replace the words of the old songs so they could be used intertribal. At a modern Powwow there are many songs today are sung in vocables, having no words. Often very special meaning is held in the songs, and to those who know the song the stories rendered are powerful, and with many songs still sung in Indian languages, many either newly composed or revivals of old songs, the culture is transmitted across generations. These Powwow songs are heartfelt reminders to the people of their old ways and rich heritage of the ancestors no gone.

Dances have always been a very important part of the life of the American Indian tribal community, and a great many of the Powwow dances seen at powwows are rooted in times past. In many cases they have origins in wars, in journeys, in hunts, and the like, all aspects of life in the old time culture, and the social dances one sees today, dances which might have had different meanings in earlier days, still are present generations later. Through the years the dance styles and regalia have changed but their meaning and importance to the Indian community has not. The beautiful and colorful regalia worn by the dancers seen at a dance today evolve over time, and new ones appear frequently. Native America is not a stagnant culture, but a vibrant and ever-changing way of life.

Many of the Powwows held across Alabama are organized by Powwow committees that work for months before the event to have everything ready. At the average powwow, the 'M.C.' is in charge of many aspects of the event, and he works with the

"A.D.", the Arena Director to keep the powwow organized and moving forward with tits schedule of events with a minimum of disruption. These two individual officers of the Powwow, along with the Powwow committee, all strive to bring the Indian people and their friends together; the chance to dance and fellowship together in the circle of the Powwow is always a joyous occasion, one that renews the heart and soul of many Indians. Most modern powwows begin with the Grand Entry, sometimes called a "Parade In", and this is the entry of all the participants who come into the arena become part of the circle of dance, something as old as mankind's presence in the southland. Some say that originally the grand entry was a parade through the town the powwow was being held in to let all attending know it was time.

During Grand Entry, everyone is asked to stand as the flags are brought into the arena, as well as when honoring songs are sung. Some of the flags carried in during the Grand Entry are the U.S. Flag which is often borne by a veteran or honor guard, differing Tribal flags, the Prisoner of War Flag, and Eagle Staffs of the Native Americans nations present at the dance. Often carried by veterans, these modern warriors hold the United States Flag in an honored position, and the American flag has a deep meaning in Indian Country; It is a way to remember brave warriors past who fought against this country in generations past to keep their tribal lands and communities safe from invaders, and it is also the symbol of the modern United States which Native American people are now a part of and who many serve in the military and who have fought for this country in wars from the Revolutionary War to Iraq.

Following the military veterans in are other honored guests of the powwow, including Chiefs, tribal Princesses, honored Elders, the powwow organizers, the men dancers, the women dancers, and others. When everyone is finally in the dance arena, the song ends and a song is sung to honor the flags and the veterans present. There will be a prayer rendered by an elder, in Indian or in English then the dancing resumes and with a few round dances the fellowship and celebration of the cherished Indian heritage gets underway!

STICKBALL

Southeastern Indian stickball could in many ways be considered to be one of the oldest "team sports" in North America and has ancient roots among many tribes who once lived in Alabama and who still do in some cases. While Stickball and Lacrosse are in some ways similar to one another, the game of Lacrosse is a traditional sport that belongs to some of the tribes of the Northern United States and Canada; Indian stickball continues in Oklahoma and parts of the Southeastern U.S. where the game originated and is an important part of the ceremonial cycle of the traditional ceremonial calendar. "The interaction between community members during stickball games teaches us all how to get along and about fair play" said Chris Adams (Tah-me Fekseko), who as a Poarch Creek Indian ceremonial leader is committed to the preservation of this important part of the southern Indian culture such as Stickball. "We have to teach our children and grandchildren these traditions so that the ways of our elders will live on" he said.

Its presence in the first recorded writings on the topic of stickball was not until the mid-17th century, as Europeans and later Americans came to live amongst the Indians of the southern lowlands and mountains. Archaeologically speaking, there is evidence that the game and its predecessors had been developed and played hundreds of years before the arrival of Europeans and was even more important in times past. Today in several communities in Alabama efforts are underway to return stickball to its place as a treasured and practiced part of the Indian heritage of the state, one unique to the continent in many ways.

Stickball artwork by Scott Sewell

THE ALABAMA INDIAN AFFAIRS COMMISSION

As we have said, the Alabama Indian Affairs Commission was created by legislative action in 1984, and it represents more than 38,000 American Indians and their families, proud residents of the State of Alabama. The Alabama Indian Affairs Commission is tasked to acknowledge the special social identity and cultural needs of Alabama's "invisible minority". As the AIAC website states, the Alabama state legislature specifically charged the Alabama Indian Affairs Commission to *"deal fairly and effectively with Indian affairs; to bring local, state, federal resources into focus...for Indian citizens of the State of Alabama; to provide aid...assist Indian Communities...promote recognition of the right of Indians to pursue cultural and religious traditions..."*

AIAC is an active advocate for the Native Americans in the state, and is a common meeting place for addressing the many issues that confront Native Americans on the state. It bridges the departments of government and the Native American people of our tribal communities. AIAC stands alone to represent the Indian people of Alabama who wish to work together in cooperation

The Indians of Alabama

with their fellow Alabama citizens while maintaining their own cultural and ethnic heritage.

HEALTHCARE

There are today nine tribes recognized by the state of Alabama as American Indian groups, and as we might expect all have unique challenges, including the health of their tribal members. The Native American population anywhere often faces unique challenges to their physical health. All the tribal governments of Alabama wish to provide the best healthcare available, and a recent survey rendered some insights into the health status of the tribes.

- ❖ The Poarch Band of Creeks* (the only Alabama Indian Tribe that is federally recognized and receives health services via the Indian Health Services Division of the Federal Government)
- ❖ The MOWA Band of Choctaw Indians* (a health care facility is located on this reservation)
- ❖ The Southeastern Mvskoke Nation
- ❖ The Echota Cherokees of Alabama
- ❖ The Cherokees of Northeast Alabama
- ❖ The Cherokees of Southeast Alabama
- ❖ The Ma-Chis Lower Creek Indian Tribe
- ❖ The Piqua Sept of Ohio Shawnee Tribe
- ❖ United Cherokee Ani-Yun-Wiya Nation

*The survey spoken of does not include these Tribes, due to their abilities to screen, monitor and assess health status and provide preventive strategies to tribal members.

In 2006, a document was designed to survey the health of the state of Alabama's American Indians. The results contained in the survey profiles the risk factors, health status and lifestyle behaviors for the seven of nine Alabama Indian Tribes.* These health findings have been published in a self-reported survey entitled, Health Survey of American Indians of Alabama 2008[3].

Though the majority of Indian tribes in Alabama lack federal acknowledgement and the in-trust reservation land that comes with that status, most are still impacted by the factors that other Native American populations experience. Alcoholism is the most well-known health problem in the Native community, and the depiction of the impacts of this disease on Indian people is familiar from the media's depiction of the 'drunken Indian'. Unknown too many though are many different physical and mental health conditions which are overly represented among Native Americans. Indeed, there are many reasons why Native Americans and Alaska Natives die younger, on average, than other Americans, and in this the state of Alabama is no exception.

---

[3] http://www.adph.org/minorityhealth/index.asp?ID=3341

Health Care

Native communities suffer more of the usual predictors of poor health, such as poverty, unemployment and a steep high school dropout rate than most other Americans, and then there is the weight of history. In the past the removal of Native American populations from their ancestral homelands, the taking of some Native American children to government boarding schools, and the specter of Jim Crow segregation all greatly impacted the lives of Alabama's Indians.

Irene Vernon is a professor at Colorado State University, and a researcher who specializes in Native American health issues. "We are the sickest racial, ethnic population in the United States," she states. "These traumatic impacts -- loss of land, loss of community, loss of family, warfare -- have been passed on from generation to generation," Vernon said. It is true that a sizable minority of Native Americans live on reservations in rural areas, as do the Poarch Creeks, the reservation populations across the country are mostly serviced by isolated clinics of the IHS. These populations deal with services often being a lengthy drive to a hospital, institutions that are usually in need of support and more funds. "The money we get for health is less than the money given to prisoners," Vernon said. "It's shamefully small, per person. One in three American Indian women is raped in her lifetime, according to the Justice Department, more than twice the national average." Among the healthcare challenges that are most pressing in Indian communities whether federal, state, or without status are diabetes, physical injuries, sexual abuse, tuberculosis, and suicide.

DIABETES

Native Americans have the highest rate of diabetes of any group in the country; according to the American Diabetes Association with consideration for age-adjustment as the Native population is somewhat younger on average. Rates of diabetes among Indians can vary though as its prevalence among Alaska Natives is lower than the national average.

Partly, the prevalence of Diabetes is related to the conditions of many reservation communities, areas of intense pockets of poverty, and suffering from limited access to healthy food in many cases. The integrity of the Native American food culture was undermined when the tribal community lost most of their lands, and became dependent on cheap and unhealthy federal rations distributed on the larger reservations. "We were a healthy people, generally, pre-contact. We had to hunt for our food, fish for our food, plant our own garden" Vernon said. "Once we were placed on reservations, and given rations -- what were those rations? The same things you give anybody you give subsidized food. Yellow cheese, if you can call it cheese."

Since 1998, there has been a federally-funded Special Diabetes Program that has made significant gains in improving the health of the diabetic. There is a mounting sovereign food movement to recover and restore the ancient agricultural practices and foodstuffs of the healthier Native American cuisine, which the Muscogee (Creek) Nation of Oklahoma as well as other tribes has been active in establishing in Native communities, with strong interest from some tribes in Alabama in replicating. Sadly, the incidence of diabetes and particularly among children in the Indian community continues to climb.

VIOLENCE and INJURIES

Though the struggle with Diabetes that many Native American communities wage is more well-known publicly, it's lesser known that more Indians die by injury by the age of 44 than from any other cause, per research from the Center for Disease Control and Prevention. In comparison to Caucasian Americans, Native people are twice as likely to die in a car crash, three and a half times more likely to die as a pedestrian. Additionally they are twice as likely to die by fire and three times more likely to drown, according to information provided by the Indian Health Service.

Many times, alcohol likely plays a role in many of these deaths, as the distance from emergency services as well. Violent crime on many reservations has significantly increased in the last decade, while off reservation it has dropped across the country in most communities. For some Indian nations, murder and violence have become normative, and are accepted as a part of life. Last year, the Department of Justice completed a two-year crime-fighting initiative on a handful of reservations modeled after the Iraq War surge. Though many of the Indian communities of the state of Alabama don't suffer from the degree of the problems that large western reservation populations do, they still face significant challenges to healthy lives.

SEXUAL ABUSE

Sexual violence is at an epidemic proportion in Indian communities across the US, and one in three American Indian women is raped in her lifetime, this according to the Justice Department, a rate which is more than twice the national average. Due in part to a lack of resources, an underfunded and unresponsive tribal police system, as well as the high rates of alcohol abuse in Indian communities, a report from 2007 from Amnesty International report stated unequivocally that "sexual violence against women from Indian nations is at epidemic proportions and that survivors are frequently denied justice."

One of the several failures of the system in this situation is that it's not possible for tribal courts to prosecute non-Native men who rape Native women on tribal reservation lands. On paper, President Obama closed that loophole when he signed the Violence Against Women Act in March. But not one tribe is currently capable of enforcing the new law, reports Frontline, though the majority of the tribes of Alabaman lack federal trust lands, the incidents of violence against women in the state are concerning. The rural nature of many of the states Indian communities mean that these are subject to the factors that are affecting both Native Americans as well as southern rural populations.

TUBERCULOSIS

For centuries, tuberculosis ravaged the Native American population, and though rates of TB have diminished significantly in the last half century, disparities are present as a study In 2008 showed; incidence of TB was still five times higher for Native Americans and Alaska Natives than for non-Hispanic whites. Of most relevance is that many of the primary risk factors for tuberculosis are simply more common in low-income communities like those many of Alabama's Indian people live in. These factors include poor nutrition, inadequate medical care, diabetes, and alcohol and tobacco use, among some.

SUICIDE

Youth suicide has become an epidemic in Indian country the last few years and Native American youth like Native American people in general, are more likely to kill themselves than any other group. They are taking own lives at triple the rate of their non-Indian peers, according to government data. The epidemic of Native suicide is a part of a constellation of issues that disproportionately affect Native people, including sexual assault, substance abuse, social isolation, joblessness, homelessness, limited mental health services, crime and incarceration.

The lives of American Indians have changed greatly in modern times from the often isolated and disenfranchised lives of generations past. In modern American life, the vast majority of American Indians in the United States are living in urban areas and not on a reservation, an environment that has many of its own healthcare threats and challenges. The policies and services of federal health care in most cases tends to focus on the needs of those Native Americans who are living on reservations, usually in rural areas isolated from population centers and the accompanying employment and educational opportunities, as well as being slated for members of federal tribes not state recognized groups. Native Americans living in Alabama are in line with this national trend, though only two of the nine recognized Indian tribe's resident in Alabama live on reservations. Many of the others suffer from many of the significant health risks that other rural Alabamians face.

Only one of the nine organized Native American groups in Alabama, the Poarch Band of Creek Indians, is federally recognized, meaning they have acknowledgement from the federal government of the direct government to government relationship between the two, and all the opportunities this provides. Because of this unique status as the only Indian tribe with federal acknowledgment in the state, one that allows them and receipt of health care and services through the federal Indian Health Services, Poarch Creek Indian tribal members have a much more affordable and somewhat broader access to medical care than other tribes in Alabama which have only state recognition or none at all.

While the MOWA Band of Choctaw Indians, one of the current nine State Recognized Tribes and the only one that has a health care facility located on their reservation has this going in its favor it still faces challenges in providing needed services. "Our people have healthcare challenges that must be addressed with the best healthcare options available", said Cedric Sunray, a MOWA Choctaw and advocate for tribal communities. These latter two tribes are able to monitor health trends and potentially prepare preventive strategies based upon health assessments and screening results, though some of the other groups face difficulties. The other state recognized tribes, as stated earlier, are profiled in a document that can be accessed online[4] and they have identified their usual source of medical care as community-based, private pay, insured, or uninsured. For many of these tribal groups of Alabama, their tribal members are located throughout the state. This unique characteristic made it difficult to systematically retrieve health data, due to the lack of a uniform health services tracking system.

Some of the Alabama's Indians health services are based upon a combination of traditional healing practices and modern Western medicine, especially in the more rural areas, with folk medicines playing a significant role in some communities. For several years, there has been a request for more inclusion of Native American people in the state of Alabama's statistical health reports. That health data for American Indians is often

---

[4] http://www.adph.org/minorityhealth/index.asp?ID=3341

aggregated with data for "others" so that real differences in outcomes have become obscured is a concern, and there is a need for true statistical data analysis of the information to get a clearer picture. The small numbers of Native American tribal populations in Alabama have made it difficult to provide a uniform and readily accessible health care system where the data can be located.

Map Mississippi Territory to 1817

ECONOMIC DEVELOPMENT

Office of Community Services

All the tribes of Alabama are seeking better ways to provide services for their members, and several tribes in Alabama are partnered with the Office of Community Services. The "Office of Community Services (OCS) partners with states, communities and agencies to reduce the causes of poverty, increase opportunity and economic security of individuals and families and revitalize communities. Our social service and community development programs work in a variety of ways to improve the lives of many." The agencies social service and community development programs work in a variety of ways to improve the lives of many.

The OCS's main goals are to serve the economic and social needs of low-income individuals and families, provide employment and entrepreneurial opportunities, promote individual economic opportunity and security through the creation of full-time and permanent jobs, support asset building strategies for low-income families and individuals such as savings, increasing financial capability and securing assets, assist community development corporations in utilizing existing funding for neighborhood revitalization projects, provide financial and technical resources to state, local, public and private agencies for economic development and related social service support activities and to provide energy assistance to low-income households. The Ma-Chis Lower Creek Indian Tribe, Mowa Band of Choctaw Indians, Poarch Band of Creek Indians, and the United Cherokee Ani-Yun-Wiya Nation all partner with the OCS on programs. Below are contacts for these:

- ❖ Ms. Nancy Carley, Vice Chief Ma-Chis Lower Creek Indian Tribe, 2950 Coffee County Road, Rm. 377 Elba, Alabama 36323 TEL: (334) 897-3207 FAX: (334) 565-3059 E-MAIL: machis@centurytel.net
- ❖ Mr. Framon Weaver, Chief LIHEAP Coordinator, Mowa Band of Choctaw Indians 1080 West Red Fox Road Mount Vernon, Alabama 36560-9639 TEL: (251) 829-5500, Ext. 106 FAX: (251) 829-5008 E-MAIL: weaver25710@aol.com
- ❖ Ms. Martha Gookin, MACO Family Services Director, Poarch Band of Creek Indians 5811 Jack Springs Road Atmore, Alabama 36502 TEL: (251) 368-9136 Ext. 2600 FAX: (251) 368-0828 E-MAIL: mgookin@pci-nsn.gov
- ❖ Ms. Gina Williamson Principal Chief, United Cherokee Ani-Yun-Wiya Nation P.O. Box 754 Guntersville, Alabama 35976 TEL: (256) 582-2333 FAX: (256) 582-2333 E-MAIL: ucanonline@bellsouth.net

Poarch Creek: Creek Indian Enterprises Development Authority (CIEDA)

CIEDA is the Creek Indian Enterprises Development Authority (CIEDA) of the Poarch Band of Creek Indians. This agency of the tribe generally works as the economic development arm of the Poarch Band of Creek Indians. The Creek Indian Enterprises Development Authority oversees the non-gaming enterprises owned by the Poarch Creek Tribe, of which there are many. CIEDA "actively supports each business achieving their specific business goals and to grow and maintain economic sustainability as put forth by the CIEDA Board of Directors and Tribal Council" according to the Poarch Band. Additionally, CIEDA executes and oversees other endeavors by the tribe including the building, construction and development projects the tribe has commissioned.

As the tribe moves forward with many economic ventures, the Wind Creek Hospitality portion of the economic development effort is the principal gaming and hospitality organization for the Poarch Band of Creek Indians. It is fully dedicated to providing a first-class customer experience to those who visit its premises. Indeed, the casinos and hotels of Wind Creek Hospitality are renowned for their geniality and refinement. Wind Creek

Hospitality operates six properties throughout the state of Alabama and the Florida Panhandle.

The impact of gaming has had for the better on the Poarch Band of Creek Indians has been extensive, with many jobs and opportunities made manifest. Indeed, as former Tribal Chairman Buford L. Rolin stated it has been crucial.

> *"It has provided our rural community with jobs — both for our Tribal members and for our neighbors. It has allowed us to add to our community's tax base, and it has provided us opportunities to educate our children, build housing and medical clinics, and improve the lives of our elderly. Our gaming business has also provided us with capital that we have used to start other businesses."*

Wind Creek Hospitality is the Poarch Creeks Tribe's principal gaming and hospitality entity. It generates a sizable and sustainable revenue stream, one that supports governmental services that contribute to the health and well-being of the Poarch Band's people. Organizationally, the organization has a five-member Board of Directors that oversees Wind Creek Hospitality and reports directly to the nine-member Poarch Creek Tribal Council.

STATE RECOGNITION VERSUS FEDERAL RECOGNITION

State recognized tribes are today becoming more present than ever on the scene of Native American politics. While Native American tribal groups, nations, and associations that have in many cases gained acknowledgement from their state by a process established under state laws for such purposes, others have not been able to for differing reasons. With growing efforts by tribal groups since the middle of the 20th century to seek acknowledgement by the federal government of their tribal sovereignty, states likewise have seen an increase in requests by groups to be recognized and some have passed legislative acts to acknowledge some tribes. The efforts by tribal groups to garner such recognition expands the resources that such groups can access as well as the acknowledgement such recognition bestows for the communities self-determination and continuity as a unique group.

Most of the groups are located in the Eastern US, though not all. Some are very well known in their long term struggles for recognition, such as the Lumbee Tribe of Cheraw Indians in North Carolina and the United Houma Nation of Louisiana, others are little known outside of their local area. While some states have recognized tribes that could be considered "landless"; Communities not having an Indian reservation or communal tribal lands held in trust like others, others have a small land base, some dating back to colonial times such as tribes in the Northeast.

Often due to the growing call for responses to the concerns of groups seeking recognition, the states have established panels, commissions or other administrative bodies to deal with Native American affairs within the state. In some states these have been controversial while in others they have garnered praise for the work they have accomplished. The growth in states recognizing groups seeking such acknowledgement has resulted in some measure from the recent phenomenon of calls for increasing self-determination and support for the preservation of unique tribal and cultural identity within some American Indian communities. Most often these are inclusive of the descendants of splintered tribes, communities whose ancestors remained in states east of the Mississippi River as many of the larger tribes were removed during the 19th century.

State acknowledgement without doubt can improve a group's access to resources as well as social standing than that of groups which lack such recognition. While state recognition is not the same as federal recognition, it is more than many had before such acknowledgement by their state was granted. While without question the federal government's acknowledgment of a tribe as a dependent sovereign nation is the highest of standards for many of the multitude ways a community can be perceived as being or not being "Indian" or Indian enough, that some states have provided laws related to state recognition, legislation that provides some limited protection of their autonomy for groups not acknowledged by the federal government. Connecticut is one example, as state law recognizing certain tribes there also protects the tribal reservations and the limited forms of self-government for state-recognized tribes there.

State recognition of tribes is as mentioned already is controversial, and It should be said that state recognition has been opposed by federally recognized tribes in most cases. Most notably due to the many hundreds of groups claiming Cherokee ancestry, the Cherokee Nation of Oklahoma opposes state-recognition of tribes who claim a Cherokee identity, as well as the countless groups lacking any recognition that also claim to be Cherokee[5].

The legal definitions of who is an Indian are many; according to a 1978 congressional survey, there were over 33

---

[5] "What is a real Indian Nation? What is a fake tribe?". Cherokee Nation. Retrieved 15 February 2016.

separate definitions of "Indian" utilized in federal legislation, and that number of definitions grows even larger when tribal enrollment statutes are included in the calculation. Federal agencies often have diverse definitions of "Indian." The National Center for Health Statistics assigns the mother's race to a child born to parents of different "races" and in the circumstance when multiracial responses to inquiries of ancestry are given, only the first race is entered. This is just one example of a very complex array of definitions defining Indian-ness found across the legal spectrum. Being a member of a federally recognized is the most easily understood and widely accepted meaning of being an Indian for many people.

Providing financial aid and other benefits to the 562 tribes currently who have this most coveted type of acknowledgement, many of these tribes received federal recognition through old treaties, Congress or the Bureau of Indian Affairs. The federal acknowledgement process through the BIA takes during the last few decades an average of 13 years, with many much longer. Some tribe's petitions can exceed tens of thousands of pages and the costs in the millions of dollars to research. As of the first decade of the new millennium there were over 300 tribes at some point in the process, with the record for the longest wait in the process going to North Carolina's Lumbee Tribe of Cheraw

Indians; their petitions have been on the table since 1888. Recent developments at the BIA have streamlined the process and hopefully this will allow for a more efficient and effective avenue for tribal groups seeking federal recognition.

There have been many complaints since the BIA crafted established guidelines for recognition in 1978, with less than 50 applications have been fully processed. The reply to questions as to why such a lengthy process, the BIA says it must be thorough with their being so much money and political mechanisms at work. Today more than ever there are hundreds of millions of dollars involved, and the accompanying controversy that that provokes. What is federal recognition at its heart that makes it so coveted for tribes to obtain? Federally recognized tribes have inherent sovereign powers which are recognized by the U.S. government, a recognition that resembles in some ways a separate state or country. The American federal government has a government-to-government relationship with federally recognized American Indian nations. This relationship is rooted in a long history of treaties, legislation, executive orders and the U.S. Constitution.

Federally recognized tribes critical of state recognition such as that extended by Alabama of other non-federally recognized groups point out that the United States federal government has a legitimation process in place for granting official recognition to American Indian nations; the Bureau of Indian Affairs. This federal acknowledgment Process requires extensive documentation, including verification of continuous existence as an Indian tribe since 1900, among others and generally takes considerable time to complete. Individual states do not have such a relationship, and it should be said that historically and legally, the individual states have been in many ways excluded from dealing with Indian nations.

The states have their own battle with federal authority in some instances, and the exclusion of the state in the federal-tribal relationship is an established trend of years. The basis for this state exclusion is established in the Constitution of the United States, effectively making state recognition unconstitutional, according to critics of state recognition. There are over hundreds of groups across the United States claiming to be Native American tribes needing recognition, but few of these groups meet the stringent requirements set forth by the Department of the Interior, Bureau of Indian Affairs Office of Federal Acknowledgement, even under the newest regulations. Some of those requirements in short are that "since 1900, it must comprise a distinct community and have existed as a community from historical times; it must have political influence over its members; it must have membership criteria; and it must have membership that consists of individuals who descend from a historical Indian tribe and who are not enrolled in any other tribe."

It is without doubt that the American Constitution, as interpreted by the Supreme Court, grants full authority regarding matters affecting the Indian tribes to the United States federal government. As defined by federal law, an Indian tribe is a group of Native Americans with self-government authority, and so this defines those groups who are acknowledged by the federal government. It would be accurate to say that most states don't have a recognition process; Around 16 states had recognized 62 tribes as of 2008. Kansas, Kentucky, Michigan, Missouri, and Oklahoma all had some type of acknowledgment though their processes of recognition that were less developed than those of the others. Most often the state legislature or relevant agencies involved in cultural or Native American affairs will establish the formal recognition for the states acknowledgement, in many cases with input by Native American tribal group's representatives, and sometimes using the already established federal criteria as somewhat of a guideline though in many this isn't the case.

One of the benefits for members of state recognized tribes, like those of federally recognized tribes, is that under the United States Indian Arts and Crafts Act of 1990 enrolled members of state-recognized tribes are eligible to exhibit and sale their wares as identified Native American artists. Koenig and Stein have examined the differences among the state recognition processes in depth, and they forward that the processes of North Carolina, South Carolina and Virginia, each having processes established by legislation into law passed by the state legislatures, as being strong models for recognition that other states should themselves use as the basis for legislation regarding to acknowledgment of Indian tribes.

In the past racial institutional and societal classifications of a person were a leading definer of their status in society and Indian Country was little different. Because the times and social realities change, for the federal authorities to continue to attempt to establish someone's Indian tribal membership using race-based criteria, i.e., blood quantum or Indian descent, such actions undoubtedly could leave the federal government in a constitutionally weak position. With the passage of time the federal government therefore has revised greatly how its regulations apportion for the distribution the benefits and rights due to American Indians.

State Recognition Versus Federal Recognition

The concerns that many of today's Native American people have over equal protections and tribal sovereignty issues have in some measure compelled the federal government to adopt a diminished role in its historic position as an arbiter of racial-based eligibility standards. Since the 1970's, this governmental policy of Native American tribal self-determination of its membership has developed. The Nixon administration played a significant role in establishing the goal of federal policy "to strengthen the Indian's sense of autonomy without threatening his sense of community. And we must make it clear that Indians can become independent of Federal control without being cut off from Federal concern and Federal support."

Most of the tribes today resident in Alabama lack federal recognition, excepting the Poarch Band of Creek. Among the tribes which have achieved state recognition the degree of infrastructure and cohesiveness vary greatly. Then unique origins and history of each group has influenced the ultimate fate that lead each to its current place as communities of Alabama. Besides the several state recognized tribes there are several more which lack even that recognition, entities whom by choice or the vagaries of history continue to struggle with their peoplehood.

Race has been a major issue in the process of state or federal recognition. Insights by Cedric Sunray, a MOWA Choctaw and other activists into the role that southern history play in the process of which tribes have recognition extended is critical of the process.

"Let us not forget the major "elephant in the room" reality that has always guided the federal recognition process concerning Black ancestry. In a recent survey of 55 continuous, identifiable, cohesive Indian communities in the Eastern and Southern regions of the United States it was found that of the 29 federally-recognized entities, all but six were found to have been listed in historical records as having mixed-white ancestry.

In the remaining six (all of who battled the BIA more so than the other 23), as well as 26 more that were not federally-recognized, it was found that all had some perceived or real association in historical accounts to have some measure of mixed-Black ancestry. As the Bureau of Indian Affairs is run by whites, mixed-white Indians, and a smaller number of racially identifiable Indians, it is clear that recognition is not about one's racial proximity to Indian, but rather one's racial distance from Black.[6] " This is no new issues concerning the perceptions of race from a non-tribal perspective playing a role in the process of acknowledgement.

---

[6] http://indianz.com/News/2013/011798.asp

State Recognition Versus Federal Recognition

In 1978 the issue was one as hot then as it is many decades later. Back then Terry Anderson and Kirke Kickingbird of the Kiowa Tribe of Oklahoma and a practicing attorney were asked by the National Congress of American Indians to delve into the federal acknowledgement issue and present their findings to the National Conference on Federal Recognition convened in Nashville, Tennessee. Their paper that was presented entitled, "An Historical Perspective on the Issue of Federal Recognition and Non-recognition" gives some insight to the issues of that moment, many of which are still present and which closed with the following:

> "The reasons that are usually presented to withhold recognition from tribes are 1) that they are racially tainted with the blood of African tribes-men or 2) greed, for newly recognized tribes will share in the appropriations for services given to the Bureau of Indian Affairs. The names of justice, mercy, sanity, common sense, fiscal responsibility, and rationality can be presented just as easily on the side of those advocating recognition."

Alabama Indians in Historical State Artwork

100 dollar of State of Alabama, Montgomery, Alabama,
1864

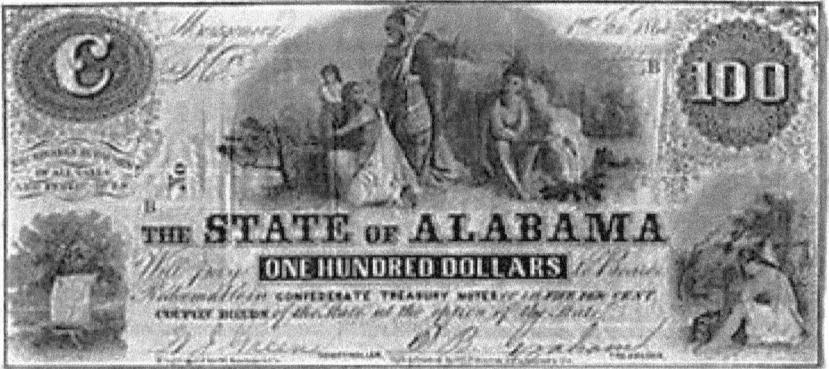

Obverse: THE STATE OF ALABAMA WILL PAY TO
BEARER - State Seal-Center Motif-Indians around campfire-
bottom Right-Topless Indian maiden sitting woefully with hand on
head, near a river-Depicting the outbreak of the small pox
epidemic.

EAGLE FEATHERS AND THE STATE RECOGNIZED TRIBES

Feathers are very meaningful in Indian culture, and the place they hold to many Native American Tribes is one of honor and prestige. The feather of an eagle isn't just something that is from a bird, it means much more; The eagle feather to traditional Native Americans is a symbolize of courage, dignity, trust, honor, strength, wisdom, power, freedom and many more things. If a person is honored as to be given one of these sacred objects, it is to be singled out for a high honor. Many Indian people hold that eagles have a special connection with the Creator Above since they fly so close to the sky. The eagle feather is used by many "traditional" Native Americans in prayer and spiritual practices, and the law provides many exceptions to federal wildlife laws regarding eagles and other migratory birds to enable American Indians to continue their traditional spiritual and cultural practices.

Under the current framework of the eagle feather law, a person of certifiable American Indian ancestry who is enrolled in a federally recognized tribe are able to legally obtain eagle feathers through established processes. When found with an eagle or its parts in their possession, those who are unauthorized can be fined up to $25,000 under the law. There are many challenges to the members of state recognized tribes in exercising their cultural identity as Native Americans who lack federal acknowledgement, and there are many that feel that the Congress should expand the eagle feather permit system to include state recognized tribes, as it does federally acknowledged tribes.

Under current laws, only enrolled members of America's 562 federally recognized tribes are allowed to obtain eagle permits and possess the feathers of eagles. This situation excludes another 62 state recognized tribes, communities who are unable to obtain eagle feathers needed to practice and preserve traditional ways of life. Native American spiritual practices have been subject to restriction and prosecution for a long time, with the persecution of its practitioners going on for centuries. In the past, even members of federally recognized tribes often had to hide their sacred possessions and practice the traditional religious ways and ceremonies in private and away from prying eyes of officials, missionaries and even fellow tribesmen who had been assimilated into non-Indian cultural customs.

Eagle Feathers and the State Recognized Tribes

Today, the members of state recognized tribes must still hide their eagle feathers or face fines and imprisonment for practicing traditional religious beliefs, in their own communities. Some scholars of the legal issues facing Native Americans such as Alexa Koenig and Jonathan Stein suggest the possibility of federally recognized tribes being given certain incentive to resist recognition of state tribes, in some cases. It would mean additional dividing up of the economic windfall that casino gaming has brought. The result of this situation is that some federal tribes, states and local communities position themselves against state tribes who are trying to gain federal recognition, or at least access to eagle feathers for traditional religious use.

As stated by the Division of Migratory Bird Management, only 1.1 percent of some 2,000,000 members of federally recognized Native American tribes have eagle permits. As many of the few dozen state recognized tribes are small, some numbering only a few hundred members, what would their inclusion in the tribes allowed feathers hurt many advocates ask? They posit that state tribes would not mean a significant increase in the number of eagle permit applications or likely decrease the number of eagles available to all for ceremonial use. An expansion to include state tribes in no way would be problematic the courts have seemed to say. In Coyote v. U.S. Fish and Wildlife

Service (1994), the authorities stated that requiring eagle permit applicants be members of federally recognized tribes "is both contrary to the plain reading of that regulation and arbitrary and capricious."

In Saenz v. Interior (2001), they ruled on the nature of the issue.

> *"whether or not a particular tribe has been formally recognized for political purposes bears no relationship whatsoever to whether or not an individual practitioner is of Indian heritage by birth, sincerely holds and practices traditional Indian religious beliefs, is dependent on eagle feathers for the expression of those beliefs, and is substantially burdened when prohibited from possessing eagle parts."*

One questions critics present is if the federal government fiduciary commitment to protect the rights of Native American tribes includes those recognized by the states. There are advocates for inclusion of state tribes in access to eagle feathers, urging the Senate Committee on Indian Affairs to support and sponsor a Religious Freedom for State Recognized Tribes Act. The bill, if approved would expand the eagle permit system to include state recognized tribes. Such an event would thereby help to protect their cultural survival and constitutional rights to religious freedom. Most importantly for eagles and current permit holders, the bill would maintain the system's current protections of eagle populations and trust responsibilities to federally recognized tribes (sourced from Indian Country Today, August 13, 2008, pp. 5.) Many of the tribal groups that are recognized in Alabama utilize eagle feathers in their traditional cultural as well as religious practices to some degree. The issue of possession of eagle feathers is one of many challenges they face as tribes without federal status.

On October 12, 2012 the Justice Department formally announced a policy that reaffirmed its intention to uphold Native Americans long established rights of eagle feather possession, as well as reaffirming its intention to prosecute people – Native and non-Native – for killing eagles without a permit from the federal Fish and Wildlife Service in the Department of the Interior, or for exchanging eagle feathers and parts for money or bartered goods or services, rather than for religious or cultural purposes. An important improvement is greater clarity about how Native craftspeople – who create regalia and sacred objects – can access eagle feathers and parts[7].

---

[7] http://fcnl.org/issues/nativeam/doj_eagles/

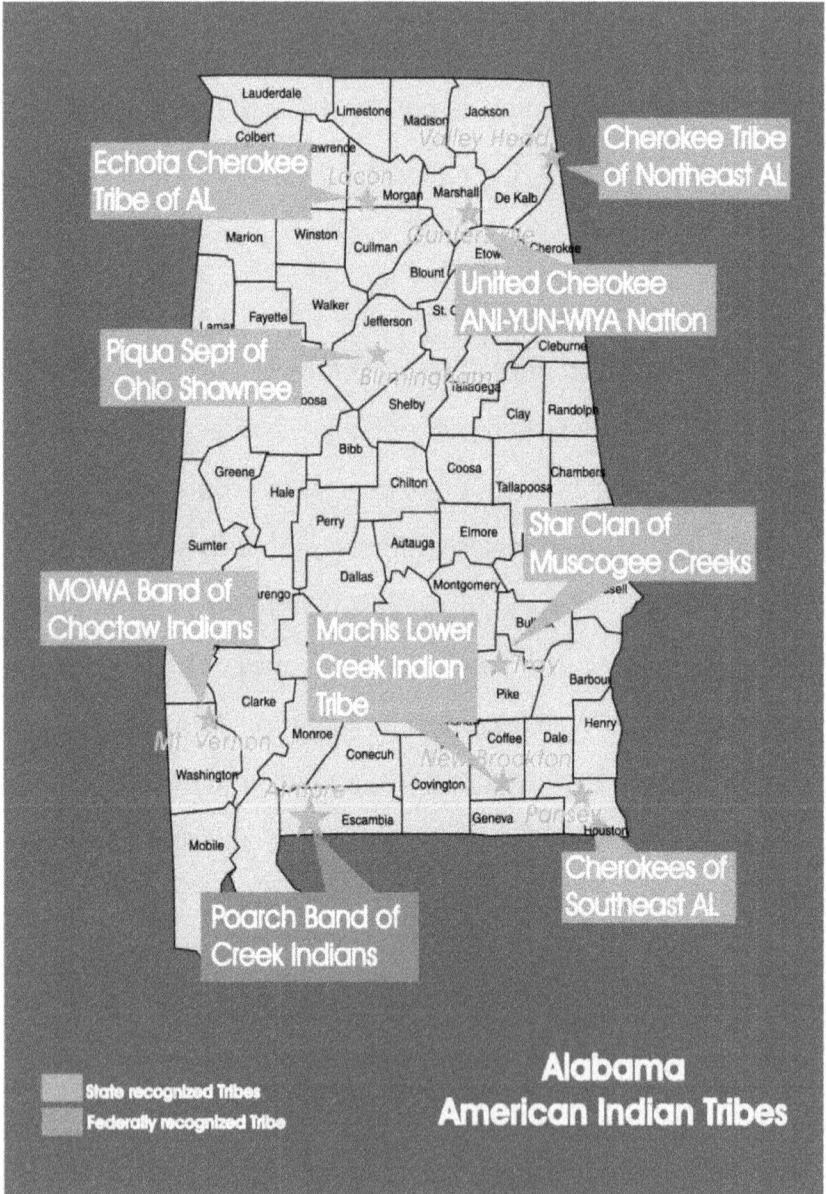

Alabama
American Indian Tribes

THE TRIBES

THE POARCH BAND OF CREEK INDIANS

The Poarch Band of Creek Indians are by far the most successful Indian tribe in Alabama, leading the way in the mid twentieth century in efforts to secure compensation for ancestral lands with the Indian Claims Commission, pioneering efforts to secure federal acknowledgment, and in bringing economic development to its reservation and population. The tribe is located in the south central portion of the state, on the Florida-Alabama state line in Escambia County, Alabama. The elected

Tribal Chairperson as of 2016 is Stephanie A. Bryan, and is reflective of the ancient Muscogee tradition of a matriarchal society in which females play a major role in community leadership and identity. The Poarch Band of Creek Indians tribal headquarters is located at 5811 Jack Springs Road in Atmore, AL 36502 The Poarch Band of Creek Indians are unique in the state as it is the only tribe in Alabama that is federally recognized.

The Poarch Band of Creek Indians is a tribe of Muscogee-speaking origin, and who live on the Alabama-Florida state border. They are a small and rugged community who are descended of a portion of the original Creek Nation, which before the genocidal removal of most Indians in the 1830's covered almost all of Alabama and Georgia. Though in that dark time many of the largest southeastern Indian tribes like the Creek, Choctaw, Chickasaw, Cherokee, and Seminole were forcible taken to the "Indian Territory", the Poarch Creeks were not removed from their original tribal lands and have lived together as a distinct and separate people since the removal, now over a century and a half ago. In the late 1700's, the Creek Nation tribal territory consisted of much of the land that is now encompassed within the modern states of southern Alabama and southwest Georgia. Divided into two groups clustered along different river systems, the two branches of the Creek Nation were two distinct communities united under one national council. The two groups would come to be called the Upper and Lower Creeks.

The Lower Towns of the Creek Nation were mostly centered in modern Georgia, clustered in villages along the Chattahoochee, Flint, and Apalachicola rivers, and further east along the Ocmulgee and Oconee rivers. This pattern of being settled along the waterways led to English settlers calling them Creek Indians. The Lower Creek towns, called Etvlwv (ee-duhl-wuh) in the Muskogee Creek language, included among their number the large towns of Coweta, Cusseta , Hitchiti, Broken Arrow, Tulwa Thlakko Apalachicola, Lower Eufala, Lower Wetumpka, Oconee, Ocmulgee, Okawaigi, Apalachee, Yamasee (also called Altamaha), Okfuskee, Sawokli, and Tamali, as well as hundreds of smaller villages. The Upper Towns were located north of the Lower Creeks and were predominately on the Coosa, Tallapoosa and Alabama rivers. Some of the Upper Creek Towns were Tuckabatchee, Abhika, Coosa, Chehaw, Hickory Ground, Hothliwahi, Hilibi, Eufaula, Wakokayi, Atasi, Alibama, Talladega, Tallahassee, Tookpafka, Coushatta, and Tuskegee among some of many.

While the heart of the Upper Creeks villages were somewhat centralized along the intersection of the Coosa and Tallapoosa Rivers near present day Montgomery, Alabama, in those days many of the people of the ancestral to the Poarch Band lived along the Alabama River, including areas from Wetumpka south to the Tensaw settlement. In the aftermath of the 1790 Treaty of New York, change began to impact the Creek Nation in a big way as Indian lands were increasingly diminished in size and over ran by squatters. When the Creeks were coerced into allowing the American government to use the existing Indian trail through the Creek lands bordering Alabama, ostensibly to facilitate American settlers journeying west to newly acquired lands following the Louisiana Purchase, disruptions and violence began to spread into the heart of the Creeks strongholds formerly free of white infiltration.

After the negotiation of the treaty, the affluent mixed blood class among the Creeks often sought to establish businesses along the Indian trails that were opening to non-Indians to accommodate travelers who were passing through the Creek Indian territory on their way westward to new lives. The trickle became a deluge when the original Indian trail was improved and eventually became the Federal Road; the numbers of non-Indians pushing into Indian lands grew exponentially and violence and disruption of Indian communities ensued. Many Creeks reacted differently to the changes, some drawing closer to Americans while others sought to resist the unwanted incursions into the Indians lands. Soon political and social fractures long present in Creek society opened into full chasms which tore at the fabric of the Creek Nation's integrity as a community.

History shows that some of the Poarch Band's Creek ancestors relocated down the Alabama River, seeking to meet a growing demand for basic services needed by the American government, and establishing new settlements, communities unique in the Creek Nation. "Friendly Creeks" as they came to be known, these forbearers of the Poarch Band of Creek community of today negotiated contracts with the American federal government, and provided help to some with whom they developed relationships, business and social; many of these families also had intermarriage with the Americans to some degree.

Many agreed to serve in roles which suited their purposes, often time acting cooperatively as guides, suppliers of food and lodging, as Creek language interpreters, others as river ferry operators and river traffic pilots, but all facilitating those traveling through the Creek Nation with easier journeys. As stated earlier, the more wealthy mixed blood class oft operated inns and taverns along the road, these "stations" often growing into settlements of their own. Some of them also operated large plantations and raised free-range cattle, adopting the southern plantation lifestyle of their non-Indian neighbors.

The Lower Creek leader Chief William McIntosh is probably one of the most well-known of these, but others such as William Weatherford are as well known. The earliest of Poarch Creek families settled land along the Alabama River from Tensaw to Claiborne and eastward along Little River, communities which would survive the coming apocalypse of the Indian removal, and seed todays Poarch Creek tribal community. The closing days of a united Creek nation saw many of the Creek towns embroiled in controversies and violent struggles in their efforts to find a way out of the trap they were in and movements commenced which would lead to war. The civil war which would plunge the Creek Nation into bloodshed was one that would take generations to heal and cost the vast expanses of lands in the south that had been Creek Indian lands for a thousand years.

American settler numbers passing through the Creek Nation's territory soon increased exponentially, a portion of these migrants stopped within the confines of the Creek Nation, often illegally, and many began settling on Indian land, squatting where they would despite efforts to have them removed by both Upper and Lower Creek chiefs. The influx of Whites into Indian lands caused tensions among the Creeks as to how best to respond, and inter-tribal violence rose steadily as the situation deteriorated into factionalism and alliances. Confrontations as well increased between Indians considered "friendly" by the Americans and others federal authorities labeled as "hostiles", the Indians whose attitudes towards the U.S. Government and its failure to keep up the agreements made soon becoming embroiled in political intrigues as control of the situation slipped into chaos.

In 1813 the situation would take a turn for the worse when a skirmish at Burnt Corn Creek between hostiles and Americans and their Creek allies would occur; the retaliatory attack for the incident at Fort Mims resulted in a massacre of white and Indian innocents alike. With relatives on both sides of the walls of the Fort Mims stronghold, the killing's that long ago day would set the course of a reckoning for Creek Nations military resistance to American authority being decided in the final battle and subsequent defeat of the Creek forces at Horseshoe Bend.

Andrew Jackson, called Old Hickory by many because of this toughness and unbending intentions to fight for what he believed in, would play major role in the fate of Native Americans in the south; many scholars agree that his Indian removal plans are one of the darkest stains on America's history, outside of the horrors of slavery. He quickly took control of Fort Toulouse, then renamed it Fort Jackson; It was here he met with mostly Friendly

Creek leaders, Chiefs and headmen who were strong-armed by the threat of the Americans military might, and who would sign the Treaty of Fort Jackson in 1814. As a result of the Treaty of Fort Jackson, the Indians and their allies resisting the will of the American manifest destiny plans would find fewer options available and a declining hope for peaceful cohabitation. Eventually the Creek Nation was illegally forced to cede the tribal lands to the Americans and most were forcibly removed from their land in the south, land that in the aftermath of this tragic event would be subsumed into Alabama. Some of those most resistant to the removal implemented after the Creek Nations defeat at Horseshoe Bend would migrate to Florida and continue the fight among the growing body of the Seminole tribe.

The removal of the Creek Nation was not the end of Creek Indians in the lower Alabama, Georgia and northern Florida area, though; it was only the end of the Creek Nation's governance of the region, as hundreds of individuals and families of Indians remained. Despite the policy of removal of Southeastern Indians to Oklahoma, many small groups from most of the larger tribes which were removed would find ways to remain in their homelands, tribes which despite the difficulties faced found ways to survive.

Across the south small groups Indians would find refuge in the North Carolina Smoky Mountains, the Mississippi swamps, the Louisiana bayous, and the thickets of the Alabama-Florida borderlands, re-establishing their communities on the fringe of the new social order. There were several Creek families in the Tensaw community who had helped the Americans by providing needed services through the years leading up to the removal. Some of these families included Dixon, Moniac, Colbert, Weatherford, Sizemore, Ehlert /Elliot, Coon, Rolin/Rollin, Marlow, Hales, Hollinger, Stiggins, and Bailey. Some of the Creek families had intermarried with Chickasaw, as well as Carolina Indians who had migrated to the area. The founding Creek families of today's Poarch Creeks and others in nearby areas were allowed to retain the lands they had been allotted as parties to the Treaty of Fort Jackson earlier.

Two important ancestors of the modern Poarch Creek community were Semoice and Lynn McGhee; they were Friendly Creek Warriors who had been unable to file for their land allotments earlier but who in 1836 had a special act of Congress that permitted land grants to them. Some of the people who were involved in this were Lynn McGhee, Semoice, Susan Marlow and Samuel Smith, and their heirs. By 1836, the Creeks who had remained behind, trapped in a deteriorating social reality, were fighting to re-establish their footing in the new south they found themselves in, one very changed in the last few decades. They were forced to accept the new state of Alabama's jurisdiction and the loss of the Creek Nation's presence in crafting lives in the Indian removal's aftermath.

The Tensaw settlement where many of the Indians were settled was becoming well populated with white people and local timber companies had been buying up large tracts of timber land for use in the growing timber industry, which left little land available for land grants. Those families receiving land grants in 1836 had little to choose from due to the increased settlement of the area by Whites. Many Creeks then chose to move inland away from the River where they had been living and into the Poarch area, settling near the Head of Perdido and Huxford area. Because of the difficulty of life at the time, the Indians developed very close family ties, with the Creek families intermarrying substantially with each other over several generations, with time a distinct group of Creeks emerged. Though they were somewhat distinct as a group even before removal they were squeezed by the social realities of the mid 1800's into a very tight knot group of people who were self-reliant and inwardly focused.

Poarch Creeks were by this time were as a group unique and was distinguished from whites and the many other descendants of Creeks who had remained in other areas after the removal. With the shadow of Jim Crow segregation falling on the south, the fortunes of the Poarch Creek would become tenuous at best. As the documentary record shows, in later years many Indians were discriminated against by whites as well as other Creek descendents in some cases. The Poarch Creek settlements became tightly clustered geographically as the 1800s passed, and the small tribe became more deeply rooted on a network of close kinship ties among dozens of families.

As the century wore on many Indians fell deeper into poverty and with the latter half of the century coming to a close racial discrimination increased. With Jim Crow at its height, the Creek families would all become poorer and their social position more isolated. For the most part Creek families in the area were finding employment, if they could find it, as farm laborers and later many worked in the pulp woods. With the increase in the social isolation the Creeks were experiencing "Indian-only" schools emerged and Native American churches appeared before the turn of the century. These were not unique to the Poarch Creeks though, as the MOWA Choctaw Community nearby also had such institutions. Poarch Creek schools, churches and other organizations are known from historic records to have been operating as early as 1908. Creeks from the several communities were interred separately from whites, with them being laid to rest in a segregated Indian burial ground called Judson Cemetery, being established on land donated by a freed slave.

In the early twentieth century, efforts became pronounced both within and outside of the Indian community to better the social and economic struggles of the Poarch Creeks. For the first time since the early 1800's, the American federal government got involved in the welfare of this small and isolated tribal groups struggles when it stepped in to defend the Indians from the Escambia County Alabama Tax Assessor's illegal taxation of the land which many of the Poarch Creek lived on, property which was Federal Trust Land in Poarch Community during the 1920's. Litigation to penalize trespassers illegally cutting timber on grant land was brought forward by the government as well, and it continued until 1925, to the benefit of the tribe. Additionally the Poarch Community hosted the presence of Episcopal missionaries, an effort that began providing assistance to the Indians in 1929.

Through the efforts of Dr. Robert C. Macy and his wife Anna, medical care and treatment became available to poorer community members. The couple, seeking to establish a religious mission to the Indians also assisted in coordinating the construction of St. Anna's Episcopal Church. This venerable institution of the Indian community is still standing today. St. John's in the Wilderness church, another important church from the same era is no longer standing but played a role in the difficult years of the early twentieth century. These community churches were not only spiritual refuges for the embattled Native Americans of the area who dealt daily with the racism and social isolation of the times, but were used as schools for the Indian children of the several hamlets of the Poarch Creek people.

The Indian community in the late 1940's began efforts to improve the community and the living conditions of the people on a legal as well as social front with increased political activism by tribal leaders, including a community boycott of the schools led by then Chief Walker and supported by Calvin McGhee and others. In 1949, the Escambia County, Alabama local government constructed a small segregated "consolidated Indian School" in Poarch. This school was slated to provide Poarch Creeks and other Indians in the area with a "separate but equal" opportunity for an education, though this opportunity only extended through the sixth grade. As former Chairman Eddie Tullis said "The families encouraged their children to marry non-Indians and to go find jobs outside the community. Once we reestablished the reservation, there's been a total reversal of that now. There is a real pride about the fact that they're Indian, has brought about a lot of that intangible benefit."

Displaying the fortitude and ambition to improve characteristic of the Creek people, the community and its leaders organized a committee to address inequalities that they faced. This movement, which was able to compel the local county school authorities to render the school bussing that allowed Native children to be able to attend junior high and high school nearby, was an important and unifying effort for the tribe. Such betterment opportunities for the Indians were also strengthened in 1970 by way of the Civil Rights movement that was sweeping the country. Linking the tribes past with recent struggles, the Poarch Consolidated School was recently restored to preserve this important aspect of the communities tribal identity.

Calvin McGhee was chosen in 1950 as a primary tribal spokesman and leader by Indians representing many families and communities, and facilitated the forming of an intertribal council called the Creek Nation east of the Mississippi. He was known far and wide for his efforts to encourage Creeks and all Indian people to step forward and organize to further the goal of restoring Native American tribal identity. Chief McGhee was a charismatic leader, and his efforts were successful in helping the Creeks to move into a more modern and cooperative form of governance.

Chief McGhee led the Poarch Community through the height of the Indian Rights movement, guiding many communities in the region towards intertribal cooperative goals until his death in 1970. He led an Indian land claims effort among the many scattered and disparate groups of Eastern Creek descendants, in Florida, Alabama, and Georgia, seeking recompense for the taking of Indian lands resulting from the illegal tactics of the Treaty of Fort Jackson.

Calvin McGhee spearheaded the struggles of the mid-twentieth century as regionally as well as nationally Native Americans raised voices together demanding self-determination and fair dealing from state and the federal government. The Creek Nation East of the Mississippi, which he established in 1950, was an important part of this rising tide of Native rights. The organization of this group, which was based at Poarch and was led by Poarch community leaders and included Indian people from several areas nearby, would in time evolve into several tribal governments, each representing the needs of the people in several areas outside of the Poarch Creeks region.

With Calvin McGhee's death, the Poarch Creek would move towards a more unified government and would establish requirements for membership more reflective of the unique identity of the Indians of the Poarch Creek Tribe. With the changing of the guard after McGhee's passing, new directions would be pursued under a newer generation of leaders from among the Poarch Creek. With time the Poarch Creek's tribal council evolved into a more formalized organization, consisting of a nine-member governing council for the Poarch community alone. Like McGhee before him, Eddie L. Tullis led the Poarch Creek Indians courageously into a new era, taking a central role in the Poarch Creek people's efforts at petitioning the United States federal government to acknowledge that the tribe had grounds for a government-to-government relationship, the foundation of tribal groups everywhere survival.

Eddie L Tullis

In a historic action the Poarch Creek finally reached the goal of federal acknowledgement and on August 11, 1984, the tribe was added to the list of federally recognized tribes, the only such tribe in Alabama. While these efforts to gain recognition did ultimately culminate in the United States Government, Department of Interior, and the Bureau of Indian Affairs extending acknowledgement that the Poarch Creek Indians did indeed exist as an "Indian Tribe" within in the meaning of federal law, its struggle to rebuild an impoverished and marginalized community had only just began. As the Poarch Creeks are the only federally recognized Tribal group in the State of Alabama, there are several other groups who in subsequent years became state recognized by Alabama, including the nearby MOWA Choctaw.

Today the 3,074 enrolled members of the Poarch Band of Creek Indians continue the fight to improve the tiny nation's long term social and economic prospects with many ventures in business, farming, and gaming underway. While over 1,000 of the Poarch creek live in the Poarch, Alabama area on or near the tribe's reservation, a small reserve located eight miles northwest of Atmore, Alabama, situated in the rolling fields of rural Escambia county, others live in other parts of the country and world, with many coming home for the annual Poarch Homecoming Powwow.

The Poarch Band of Creeks is the only tribe in Alabama that is federally recognized, and today the decades since acknowledgment in 1984 have seen the Poarch Creek community grow, and with it many Indians from other tribes have come to live in this beautiful corner of Alabama. Lakota, Seminole, Brotherton, Choctaw, Catawba, Chitimacha, and dozens of other tribes have community members who are today among the many thousands of Poarch Creek in the area around Atmore. The Homecoming Powwow and other events are popular and draw tens of thousands of people to the reservation. The future is bright for this dynamic and strong tribe.

Chris Adams

Contact Information

Poarch Band of Creek Indians, Stephanie A. Bryan, Tribal Chair

5811 Jack Springs Road Atmore, AL 36502 (251) 368-9136

www.poarchcreekindians.org

ECHOTA CHEROKEE TRIBE OF ALABAMA

Stanley Trimm is the Chief of the Echota Cherokee, and this tribe is located at 410 Main Street West in Glencoe, AL. The Echota Tribe continues to grow in its service to its members, and has obtained tribal land in St. Clair County, Cullman County, and around Smith Lake, Alabama. A tribal office was opened in Falkville, Alabama to serve tribal members who live there. Like many of the tribes of Alabama, the Echota Cherokee host annual dances, powwows, and gatherings that are held to celebrate the continued growth of the tribe. "The identity of the Echota Cherokee is an important part of my life and of my family" said one young woman from the Chavers family, "we are proud to be Cherokee and from Alabama".

HISTORY

According to Echota tribal history, the members of the Echota Cherokee Tribe of Alabama are the descendants of Cherokees who escaped the Trail of Tears by hiding in the mountains, or who were able to escape during the march, or whom returned after being brought to Indian Territory in the west. Tribal elders passed down the identity within the community, and their descendents say that the Echota Cherokee language and culture were kept hidden and secret from outsiders, for fear that if someone would find out they would be taken to Indian Territory and everything they had would be taken by the state of Alabama. Tribal ancestors were often racially harassed and in order to hide their non-white ancestry they would claim to be "Black Dutch" or similar names and many families share stories of elders taught to keep their skin covered with hats and long sleeves at all times, in order to avoid being any darker than they already were, according to the tribes oral history.

During the late 1970s the Echota people whose ancestors had been forced to hide were able to start coming out as being Native Americans. Echota Crafts, stories, and tribal language were shared at gatherings of the people. In 1980 it was decided that a formal name and entity needed to be established besides the informal Cherokee identity that had been known up until then. At a meeting in Opelika, Alabama on March 16th the name Echota was chosen and the phoenix became the tribal symbol. It was thought by some of the tribal members that since the Echota Cherokee were rising from the ashes of burned villages and the trail of tears to come back and reclaim what they had almost lost, it was an appropriate symbol of the tribe as a group.

GAINING STATE RECOGNITION

Members of the Echota Cherokee Community were instrumental in the creation of the Alabama Indian Affairs Commission. After the Echota Cherokee tribe of Alabama filed Articles of Incorporation in 1981, Principal Chief Joseph "Two Eagles" Stewart sought to gain legislation through the state to create an Alabama Indian Affairs Commission. It was thought this would facilitate the seven tribes already organized some type of State Recognition. Every year when the State Legislature went into session, Echota members would go to Alabaster, AL., there to be met by Principal Chief Joseph Stewart and his wife Charlotte. Together they went to Montgomery to lobby the Legislature for an Indian Commission and State Recognition, a task that took place three days a week, every week the Legislature was in session.

Those who were involved in this effort remember there would at times be a van load along for the trip and other times less. Most of the Echota people involved in the effort would do what they were able to and most would make the trip as often as they could. They would tell one another to give it your all, do your best as often as you can and good would come of their efforts, and ultimately they were right. Echota members were in the State Capitol often, speaking with their local Senators and Representatives about the needs of the Indian people of the state and the importance of a commission to address these Native concerns.

After years of perseverance by members of the Echota community their hard work and efforts would see results when in 1984 the Davis - Strong Act was passed by the House and the Senate of Alabama. For the first time in generations, this Bill gave a voice in government to Native Americans in the state when it created the Alabama Indian Affairs Commission. The bill also extended recognition by the State of Alabama to the seven tribes who had joined the Echota in efforts to gain political representation as Indian groups for their people in the halls of state governance. The phrase, "Progress through Indian Unity" was added to the logo, reflecting the spirit of cooperation and goodwill the movement to gain recognition had created among the tribes and with the state.

ECHOTA PEOPLE IN THE NEWS

❖ Echota Cherokee people continue to show their strength as a people, with garnering acclaim. The 2008 Native American Music Award Winner "Golana " Echota Cherokee member Scott Cunningham aka "Golana "is an 8 time "NAMA" Award Nominee and a member of the Deer Clan West. He received the Native American Music Award for Best Instrumental Recording for his CD "Mirror Lake", and continues to enchant with his musical and creative abilities.

❖ "Miss Indian Alabama 2009" was an Echota Cherokee tribal member, Charmin Richardson who met with Alabama Governor Bob Riley and who continues to represent and advocate for Native American people and issues.

❖ Another Echota Cherokee tribal member who has garnered attention is Ron Warren . The 2010 NAMA 2 Time Nominee is a composer/arranger as well as a performer on both Native American flutes and keyboards. His creative efforts in a wide range of media have been heard in multiple venues throughout the United States and Europe. The artist has been acclaimed by many including the Washington Post, which has praised his "pensively evocative music" as well as his "expressive and highly energetic" performances. Mr. Warren's work has been encouraged and supported by numerous organizations and ensembles, including the American Composers Forum, Meet the Composer, Inc., American Indian Heritage Education Association (AIHEA) and the Contemporary Music Forum, and he has emerged as one of the most versatile and dynamic Native American flute players in the country. He has recently performed on both flutes and keyboards with renowned world musicians such as Joseph Fire Crow, Coyote Oldman, Ash Dargan, Jeff Ball, Peter Phippen, Mary Youngblood and R.C. Nakai, as well as other top performers. He was the first Native American flutist to perform at the Inter-American Development Cultural Center in Washington, DC, has been featured on Montgomery County Television, has recently performed and been a featured composer at the National Museum of the American Indian as well as performing for Pope Benedict XI at the Nationals Ballpark , both in Washington DC.

Contact information:

Echota Cherokee Tribe of Alabama, Tribal Leaders Stanley Trimm, Charlotte Hallmark
410 Main Street West, Glencoe, AL 35904 (256) 492-8678
P.O. Box 830 Vinemont, AL 35179
 E-Mail: stanleyandhelen@bellsouth.net
 www.echotacherokeetribe.homestead.com

Cherokee of NE Alabama

CHEROKEE TRIBE OF NORTHEAST ALABAMA

The Cherokee Tribe of Northeast Alabama is led by Chief Stan Long and is headquartered at 113 Parker Drive in Huntsville, AL. It is one of several Cherokee groups in Alabama and is like its peers in working to preserve the unique identity of the Cherokee who remained in the state after the removal of the majority of the Cherokee to the west.

History

The Cherokee Tribe of Northeast Alabama has an enrolled membership of over 3,000 people, though some of these reside in other areas, including Canada, Japan and even Africa according to the tribe. The Cherokee Tribe of Northeast Alabama is one of the nine tribes recognized by the State of Alabama, and it has with representation with the state government through its participation in the Alabama Indian Affairs Commission. The Cherokee Tribe of Northeast Alabama is governed by a Tribal Council, a body that is made of seven Council Representatives and a Secretary/ Treasurer. The tribal council adjourns every three months in their work on behalf of the membership, and the tribe additionally has a Circle of Elders as well as a Warrior Society. The tribe was incorporated on December 11, 1980 with Dr. Lindy Martin serving as Principal Chief initially. The tribe was initially known as the Cherokees of Jackson County, but as the tribal membership grew, the name of the group was changed to Cherokee Tribe of Northeast Alabama.

The Cherokees of Northeast Alabama support and hosts two American Indian Festivals annually in the town of Grant, Alabama, gatherings which are held on the third weekend of May and the second weekend of September. Most of the events sponsored by the tribe are open to the public. Governmentally, tribal leadership elections are held every three years for all offices. As of 2016, the Chief of the Cherokee Tribe of Northeast Alabama Warrior Society was Butch "Sky Warrior" Steakley, having been appointed by past Chief Jim Pell. He serves at the discretion of the Principal Chief, and the Warrior Society of the Cherokee tribe of Northeast Alabama often represents the tribe at all tribal functions. Dr. Tony McClure, PhD. a Cherokee Tribe of Northeast Alabama tribal member has written a book to assist in Native American Genealogy entitled "Cherokee Proud" which is available at various festivals and bookstores or at 4040 Booth Road, Somerville, TN 38068 or by E-mail from CheroProud@aol.com.

Alabama is rich in Cherokee history including some of the first written Cherokee laws being enacted in Alabama. Several of the earliest Cherokee delegations to Washington D.C. included Alabama Cherokees. The Cherokee Tribe of Northeast Alabama considers their tribe to be 'Cherokee descended' as a people, and state that their rolls are open for anyone that can document their Cherokee ancestry. Inquiries regarding such can be addressed by the tribe's genealogist, Ms. Judy Huntington, located at the Cherokee Tribe of Northeast Alabama, PO Box 66, Grant, AL 35747. The Cherokee Tribe of Northeast Alabama (formerly known as the Cherokees of Jackson County, Alabama) according to the BIA has submitted a Letter of Intent to Petition for federal recognition dated September 23, 1981, a status which it has not yet achieved though it continues to work towards all its goals.

Contact Information

Cherokee Tribe of Northeast Alabama, Stan Long, Chief
113 Parker Drive Huntsville, AL 35811 (256) 426-6344
E-Mail: stan.long11@gmail.com
www.cherokeetribeofnortheastalabama.com

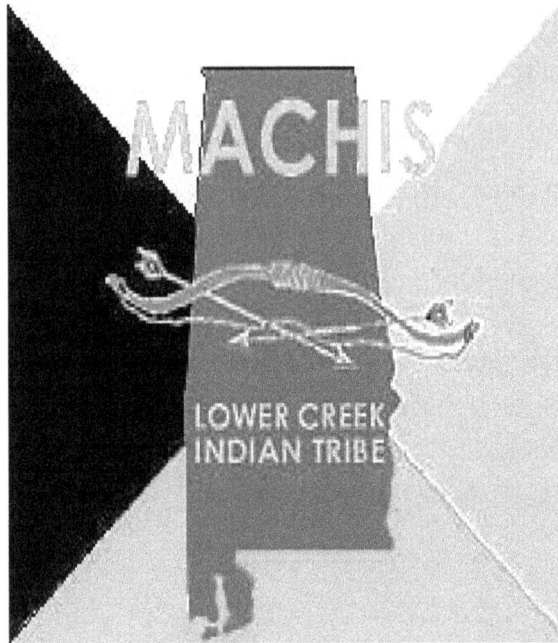

MaChis Lower Creek

MA-CHIS LOWER CREEK INDIAN TRIBE OF ALABAMA

James C. Wright is the Chief of the MaChis Creeks, and the tribe is headquartered at 64 Private Road 1312 in Elba, Alabama. They are one of several groups of Indian people in Alabama with roots in the historic Creek Nation, which was forcibly removed to Indian Territory west of the Mississippi in the 1830's. More than some other state recognized tribes in the state the Ma-Chis are a very active group in the area of economic development, with a thriving and successful track record of seeking and securing opportunities to create growth, jobs, and value not only for their tribal members, but for everyone in the state. The tribal Economic Development Committee of the Ma-chis Lower Creek Indian Tribe along with James Wright, the Tribal Chief, has made significant gains in their economic ventures. One is the Ma-Chis Lower Creek Indian Tribe Enterprises Inc. (ma-chis lcite) is a chartered tribal business corporation created for the purpose of promoting the economic development and long-term financial viability of the Ma-Chis Nation.

The Ma-Chis Nation is the sole owner of a SBA certified 8a Tribal Corporation, (a wholly Native American owned and operated corporation), which together with the support and infrastructure of their associates are eligible for Direct Award contracts and as well are exempt from the $3 million dollar threshold. This is economic development on a large scale indeed! This business offers a wide range of services including scheduling, government, family housing, maintenance, estimating, protective force services / security guard services, construction management, environmental and land rehabilitation, project management, projects recycling / refuse services electrical telecom and security systems, underground utilities, preventive and emergency maintenance, steel assembly facilities maintenance, technical consulting, design / build construction, electronics design and manufacturing.

Today as in years past the tribe continues multiple efforts at economic and social development, as the Elba Clipper reported in 2012. The "MaChis Lower Creek Indian Tribe of Alabama holds groundbreaking ceremony", the public read of an Alabama Indian tribe moving forward with its efforts at tribal development and cultural restoration. The tribe's groundbreaking ceremonies for a permanent church building to house the MaChis Lower Creek Indian Tribe of Alabama was successful. The facility located at 2950 County Road 377 was facilitated by the leadership of tribal council members including Elizabeth Hughes, Vice-Chief Nancy Carnley, Jr. Johns, Chief James Wright, Dr. Joe Johnson, Wayland Shackleford, Larry Grant and Reverend James Hattaway. Since that time the tribe has continued to develop and move ahead with its plans for growth and economic opportunity and cultural preservation of the MaChis Creek Indian identity.

In 1988 the MaChis tribe was found ineligible for federal recognition after a lengthy process to try and secure acknowledgement by the Bureau of Indian Affairs, a discouraging result that they shared with several groups which petitioned from the region in that time who also received negative findings in the 1980's. The MOWA Choctaw and the MaChis Creeks have both weathered this setback with balance, vigor and a renewed effort to addressing their people's needs without federal recognition.

Contact Information

MaChis Lower Creek Indian Tribe of Alabama
202 North Main Street Kinston, Alabama 36453
(334)565-3207
 Email: machis@centurytel.net

Ronnie F. Williams, Chief

SOUTHEASTERN MVSKOKE NATION

Formerly known by several tribal names in years past on their journey to fully restore their tribe to strength and health, on June 14, 2014, the Lower Creek Muscogee Tribe East, Star Clan, Inc., officially changed its name to the Southeastern Mvskoke

Nation, Inc.[8] Ronnie F. Williams is the Tribal Chief of this group
and the tribe is headquartered at P.O. Box 296 in Midland City,
AL. This is one of the oldest formally organized groups among the
state recognized tribes of Alabama, and one that has played an
important role in the formation of the state recognition that
many tribes in Alabama now benefit from.

History

The Southeastern Mvskoke Nation calls itself a part of the
Lower Muscogee Creek Indians, the "People of the One Fire", and
is a part of Alabama's well known Creek Indian heritage, like
several other tribes. The tribe is a non-profit organization, and is
one of nine state recognized Indian Tribes. After decades of
struggle to organize and develop state recognition today, the
Southeastern Mvskoke Nation continues the traditions of their
Muscogee ancestors by promoting peace and understanding of
the Native American lifestyle through continuing education. In
addition to one of the largest Indian Education program in the
State of Alabama, the tribe maintains have several "on-going"
projects, which serve to preserve the Native American heritage,
and provide a positive influence in surrounding communities.

---

[8] (including the Star Clan of Muscogee Creeks, Lower Creek Muscogee Tribe
East, Star Clan, and Yufala Star Clan of Lower Muscogee Creeks)

As they met the twenty-first century and its challenges, the tribe is dedicated to making the dream of a strong tribe an established reality. The efforts for continuing acquisition of tribal lands will enable the tribe to expand its educational base as well as provide areas for an authentic "Living" Creek Indian village, a central meeting hall and museum, and a dedicated wildlife preservation area. Goals including the construction of an "Outdoor Classroom" and on-site camping facilities for the tribe have had many members working hard.

The tribe holds regular monthly meetings in Pike County Alabama (Troy), designed to provide cultural and educational opportunities for all of their tribal members. Cultural activities are highlighted each year with the observance of the following Native American activities: Green Corn/Homecoming Festival and Annual Tribal Pow-Wow

Contact Information

Southeastern Mvskoke Nation, Ronnie F. Williams, Chief
P.O. Box 296,
Midland City, AL 36350
(334) 983-3723

CHER-O-CREEK INTRA-TRIBAL INDIANS, INC. (AKA CHEROKEES OF SOUTHEAST ALABAMA)

Violet Parker Hamilton is the Chief of this tribe which is headquartered at 1315 Northfield Circle in Dothan, AL. They have been steadily working to bring the tribe to strength and unity in their quiet corner of southeastern Alabama. The tribe's presence along a major travel corridor to the Florida beaches presents it with opportunities for economic development, and it is today moving forward with efforts to strengthen the future for its people.

HISTORY

The Cherokees of Southeast Alabama are also known as the Cher-O-Creek Inter-tribal Indians, Inc. and these intra-tribal Indian people's ancestral bloodlines, are according to their history made up of ancestry of more than one bloodline originating with at least a couple of the "Five Civilized Tribes" indigenous to the State of Alabama; primarily Creek and Cherokee. Many of Cher-O-Creek tribal members believe that they have both Creek and Cherokee bloodlines in their ancestry and this does shape the way they see their identity, as an "intra-tribal" Indian people.

The narrative of their genesis shared by the Cher-o-Creek tribe is that in the 1820's and 1830's, the United States government strong-armed the Southeast Indians to cede to the Americans their ancient tribal homelands and eventually made the tribes move westward to Indian Territory. The several tribes that didn't go along with these removals were forced to go by the Indian Removal Act and armed force. Despite this terrible tragedy, there were members of the Five Civilized Tribes who were able to avoid the Indian Removal. Many of these Indians, by escaping into the forests and mountains, were able to remain. Through marriage to white settlers and trappers/hunters, they established new homes and families.

The Indians of Alabama

Some of the ancestors of today's tribe would tell other people they were "Black Dutch" or "Black Irish" to hide their mixed ancestry. Though they were denying their American Indian bloodlines, many still felt connected to this identity. The speaking of their native language faded with the years, not transmitted in some cases to avoid their children from being heard speaking their native language and being subjected to the racism prevalent at the time. According to the tribes oral history, all the children were "cautioned to avoid answering questions when asked about their families", and many were able to avoid the heavy hand of prejudice that lay over the south. As time passed, the tribal traditions of the group say that general society became more acceptable and tolerant of them living in their communities, and Christian missionaries encouraged the Indian people to affiliate with their churches.

Acceptance and tolerance by their fellow Alabamians was the beginning for a new era, one where the Indians began to feel less afraid of their non-Indian neighbors. Indian people soon began to meet and to share again what they could remember of the Native American heritage. The community began to have group meetings, and from that start the rebuilding of their identity and culture as Native American descendents began, and as the years have passed, the Cher-O-Creek citizen's pride in their Native American ancestry and heritage has returned.

Contact Information

Cher-O-Creek Intra Tribal Indians, Violet Parker Hamilton, Chief
Po Box 717, Dothan, AL 36303
1315 Northfield Circle, Dothan, AL 36303 (334) 596-4866
E-Mail: vlt_hamilton@yahoo.com

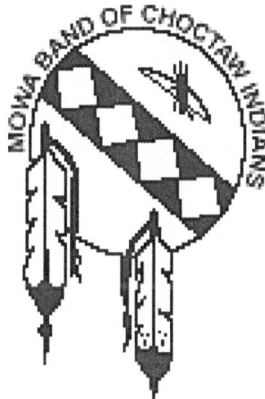

MOWA BAND OF CHOCTAW INDIANS

The MOWA Choctaw are truly a unique and spirited people, long known for their independence and vigor as a distinct community. Chief Framon Weaver is the leader of the modern MOWA Band of Choctaw Indians, ones of the state's oldest recognized Indian groups, and one with an amazing history and identity which has been well established over the last 150 years. He and the past tribal leaders have worked unceasingly to better the lives of the MOWA Choctaw people. The tribe is headquartered at 1080 Red Fox Road in Mount Vernon, AL. and is very active among state Indian affairs.

Today the Mowa Band of Choctaw Indians consists of 3,600 tribal members who are situated in Mobile and Washington County, Alabama, and the group has a state tribal reservation that is situated on 300 acres of land in Mt. Vernon, Alabama. The MOWA Choctaw community and its small state reservation located near the Mobile and Tombigbee rivers, near the small southwestern Alabama communities of McIntosh, Mount Vernon and Citronelle, centered north of the city of Mobile.

The tribe provides numerous services for its tribal members, and is governed by a Chief and eleven members of the MOWA Tribal Council, and the tribe does today have a total population of around 5,000 people. The tribe has a state reservation unlike many of the other state recognized tribes of Alabama. Cedric Sunray, a MOWA tribal member put it in perspective in relation to other states.

> *"The MOWA Band of Choctaw Indians resides on one of only nine state-recognized Indian reservations in the United States. Of the nine oldest Indian reservations in the*

country, eight are occupied by historic "non-federally" recognized tribes. The concept that only federally-recognized tribes reside on Indian reservations (though many do not) is not only a misnomer, but is also one that portrays a fictitious historical account."

Currently, Chief Framon Weaver and eleven elected Tribal Council members govern the operations of tribal affairs for the MOWA Choctaw. The Tribe's jurisdiction is exercised to the fullest extent through the Tribe's constitution and sovereign powers in its efforts to strengthen and progress as a tribal community that has faced countless hurtles over the last 150 years to become the vibrant community it is today. The Tribal Council provides services primarily to Mobile County and Washington County areas. However, services are provided throughout other continental United States areas if permitted by law or program regulations. The MOWA people also have a tribal court settles any litigation between tribal members.

The religiousness of the MOWA Choctaw is most expressed in the Catholic, Holiness, and Protestant, traditions of Christianity. As a tribe they are related culturally to other southeastern Indian groups such as the Mississippi Choctaw, Muscogee (Creek), Chickasaw, Seminole, Cherokee, and belong to the Muskogean language family. The MOWA Choctaw have many groups which contributed to their origin as a modern Indian people.

> "Over the years over 20 federally-recognized tribes have intermarried with the MOWA Choctaw and they and their descendants reside on both reservation and privately held Choctaw lands in the communities of and surrounding Mt. Vernon, Citronelle, and McIntosh, Alabama. These tribes include the Navajo, Cherokee Nation, Kiowa, White Mountain Apache, and many others."

This statement that was said by Cedric Sunray of his people's ancestors[9] could be said of many southeastern groups of Indian people. Today as well there are many MOWA Choctaw tribal members who also reside in the state of Oklahoma, in part due to their intermarriage with Indian communities located there. The tribe claims to descend from small groups of Choctaw and other Native Indians remnant in Mississippi and Alabama, Native Americans who avoided removal to the west to the Indian Territory in present-day Oklahoma, in the 1830's and who found refuge in the area where they now call home. For many years the MOWA Choctaw have attempted to gain federal recognition but have yet to succeed.

---

[9] http://www.indianz.com/News/2013/011791.asp

Wilford "Longhair" Taylor a longtime elected Chief of the MOWA Band of Choctaw Indians

History

Alabama had been inhabited for countless thousands of years by diverse indigenous peoples with a wide range of cultures including the highly developed Mississippian culture, which is believed to be formative to the historical tribes of the Muskogean-speaking Creek and Choctaw. The region would later be ruled by various European powers including French, Spanish, British, and eventually the Americans. Many of the Indians who came to the area were refugees seeking security after the Creek War of 1813-1814 as well as Choctaw who refused to be removed to the Indian Territory in 1830. These Indians were able through the Dancing Rabbit Treaty to stay as state and American residents; on the condition they surrendered their Choctaw Nation tribal membership.

According to the MOWA tribal history, around 1835 the Alabama state government built the Weaver Indian school at Mount Vernon, Alabama, but the years preceding the American Civil War, were difficult as the Choctaw were at risk of possible removal west by the federal government, as well as whites intent on raids to get slaves. The period of the late 1800's was on in which some MOWA intermarried with European American neighbors, from oral history accounts and the historic records. The communities of the MOWA have multiple references in the historical records, with the presence of Choctaw Indians well documented in this part of Alabama, and there were Native American schools in the counties where the MOWA lived.

The MOWA were a part of an increasing Native American activism taking place across the Unites States. A movement spread across the country of advocacy and political and cultural renewal. The MOWA Choctaw, like many other Indians during the "Native American renaissance" of the 1960's and 70's, insisted on their right to self-identification and recognition by the state and federal governments of their peoplehood. In 1979, the Choctaw community organized into a formal government and tribal body to be known as the MOWA Band of Choctaw Indians. Their tribal name of "MOWA" is a contraction of Mobile and Washington, the two counties which they as a group are centered.

The Band's central tribal office is located in the town of McIntosh. Their goals of self-determination were partially fulfilled on their becoming the first State Recognized Tribe by the State of Alabama in 1979. The newly State Recognized MOWA Choctaw purchased their first 160 acres of land in south Washington County in 1983, property which was recognized as a reservation by the state of Alabama. The MOWA are a unique group that is descended from several Indian tribes in their ancestry; Choctaw, Creek, Cherokee, Mescalero, and Apache as well as others contributed to today's MOWA tribe.

Their annual cultural festival, an event which includes social dances, southeastern Indians stickball games, a MOWA Choctaw princess contest, as well as a popular inter-tribal pow-wow, is held on the third weekend of June on the MOWA Choctaw's state reservation. Indian people from all over the state attend the annual event and all have a great time according to many. The MOWA Choctaw sought not only state acknowledgement, but also petitioned the federal government for recognition as an Indian tribe. In 1994 the Bureau of Indian Affairs denied the MOWA Band of Choctaw's federal recognition petition.

The Choctaw note numerous historical factors have made it difficult for them to satisfy BIA requirements, and they continue to try to find a path to federal acknowledgement. Despite the lack of federal recognition, the ethnic identity of the MOWA is well known in the state of Alabama and has been since the 1800's. The MOWA Choctaw have preserved their identity by cultural practices through the years.

> *"The strongest evidence of the MOWA Choctaws' Indian ancestry is not, however, found in written documents; it is found in their lives. Their ancestors passed to them their Choctaw Indian and African identity and traditions, persevering and preserving their heritage despite a long history of persecution and discrimination. Interviews with elders reveal stories of survival by hunting, fishing, trapping, and sharing the kill; rituals related to marriage, birth, and death; customs associated with gardening, medicinal plants, logging, dipping turpentine, and restricted communication with outsiders; and ancestral relationships told generation to generation. Despite*

hardships, the Choctaw Indian community north of Mobile persisted as a system of social relationships solidified within ceremonial gathering areas, churches, schools, cemeteries, and kin-based villages. Reduced in numbers, and increasingly a dominated minority in their own homeland, the ancestors of the MOWA Choctaws made new alliances."

The historian Jacqueline Anderson Matte offered during her work with the tribe to document their history with the BIA shows a long struggle for equality. Today, the MOWA Choctaw Tribe is doing well, despite its unsuccessful struggle for federal recognition. It has several departments and committees that operate within the tribal organization to provide leadership and quality of life to tribal members. Each of these departments or committees generates funding, principally from grants, fundraisers, and donations. These monies are slated to foster economic as well as social development for the tribe, and to facilitate energy, housing, and food development as well. The principle department within the Tribe is the MOWA Choctaw Housing Authority, an organization whose primary role is to secure funds from the U.S. Department of Housing and Urban Development in order to build houses for tribal members.

The tribe also has an Industrial Development Department that is managed by a 7 member appointed board whose primary responsibility is promoting economic development for the tribe. The MOWA Choctaw Services, LLC is an important component of this development. As well the Athletic Department is slated with the primary responsibility focused on health and recreation for tribal members. The Pow-Wow Department has a primary responsibility is to promote tribal heritage and cultural events especially the annual Powwow.

They host an inter-tribal pow-wow that occurs on the second weekend of October on the tribal reservation land in Alabama. This annual tribal event showcases the MOWA peoples pride in their community and has a cultural festival, which includes Choctaw hymn singing, Choctaw social dancing, stickball games, and a Choctaw princess contest. Tribal members and visitors enjoy the many events as well as the delicious Native American food, soulful Native drums and dancing, craft demonstrations, and a variety of entertainment and fun.

The MOWA Tribal Police Department provides security to tribal events and the tribe's property. The tribe also has a Museum Department who has the important responsibility to gather, restore, exhibit, and maintain tribal artifacts as well as to maintain the historic building that houses tribal artifacts. After many years of struggling with challenges of the past including the Indian removal, Jim Crow Segregation, poverty, and the onset of modernity, the MOWA Choctaw people are now on the solid ground that they have so long strived for. They have a strong, responsive tribal government, a land base and reservation with their own HUD and other programs, and are going into the future with a generation of educated and savvy leaders stepping forward.

Contact Information

MOWA Band of Choctaw Indians, Chief Framon Weaver
1080 Red Fox Road
Mount Vernon, AL 36560 (251) 829-5500
E-Mail: lebaronbyrd@aol.com
www.mowa-choctaw.com

PIQUA SHAWNEE TRIBE

Gary Hunt is the Chief of this small tribe, which is headquartered at 3412 Wellford Circle in Birmingham, AL. While among the more recent additions to the list of Indian tribes in Alabama, they have long been working to secure a place among the tribal nations of the Yellowhammer State as an equal.

History

While many people associate the Shawnee people with the Ohio Valley and best know this tribe through its most famous son the famous war Chief Tecumseh, the name is not unrepresented in the Cotton state. Labeled as nomadic by some researchers, Shawnee people were very widespread in their movements through the centuries, and archaeologists have found evidence of Shawnee communities in many regions. They were prone to moving about in many areas in different parts of North America, settling in various places for a period of time before moving again. The area which today is called Alabama has long been the home of many Shawnee people and some researchers believe that it is possible that Shawnee people have resided in Alabama for longer periods of time than any other geographic region.

While there are some academic sources that set the date of 1685 as the first documentarily evidenced presence of Shawnee settlement in Alabama, Piqua Shawnee Tribal oral history states that the group may have been in the area much longer than that; archaic burials have been unearthed that showed the use of some burial styles common to Shawnee culture, interments located in several parts of the state according to the tribe. Manuscripts from the colonial era, including early French and English maps indicate the presence of several Shawnee communities in what could be considered the lands of the Upper Creeks in Alabama. The remains of such a village were located near the present day city of Talladega. This settlement was sometimes listed as Shawnee Town, and another such settlement was near Sylacauga.

The records of the past reveal that as early as 1750, French officials took a census that made mention of the Shawnee at Sylacauga. Additionally this report enumerated another Shawnee town, a community called Cayomulgi, currently spelled Kyamulga town, which was located nearby. This Kyamulga village was also found included in an 1832 census. A decade after the French mention of Sylacauga, an English census enumerates Tallapoosa Town, which was also named by Marbury in a 1792 census, and many believe these to indicate Shawnee communities. Again, French military records also mention a Shawnee presence at Wetumpka near Fort Toulouse, in a region long thought to be mainly Creek Indians.

Many of these alleged "Creeks" were not of the same tribe or nation, and ties between the Creek and Shawnee are well documented across colonial times and later. Every Indian group maintained their own unique identity, while living side by side with their neighbors in intertribal cooperation against common threats. Tecumseh mother was known to be affiliated with the Creeks and an important town among the Creek Nations number, the Tukabatchee Town was known to have deep ties to the Shawnee historically as Tecumseh himself visited to garner support for his struggle against the loss of Indian lands.

A careful study of southeastern history will reveal that not all settlers agreed with Andrew Jackson's removal policy, there being many who sheltered and protected Indian people who were their neighbors during the round-up of the Native Americans in Alabama, and while many people did not escape the removal, some did and their descendants are today still struggling to survive as peoples. Finding a racial hostile society around them in the years after the Indian removals as well as poverty at their doors, many Indians retreated into an insular way of life.

It is said that after the turmoil of the enforced removals had subsided some families of Indians returned to the areas they once had lived in, according to the oral histories of their descendant's. Many of these newly landless families chose to live in outlying and isolated rural areas far from population centers, areas where there was little government scrutiny and their neighbors weren't too curious as to people's origins. While a lot was lost during these dark times, family histories and old ways were passed down to subsequent generations.

Today

In the 21st century, there are many who proudly call themselves the descendants of the ancient communities of Shawnee who still call Alabama home. Many of their family stories are varied as to how they came to remain in the state even as most Indians were forcibly removed. These stories tell of many Indians who avoided walking the Trail of Tears towards the setting sun, relating how there were some Indian families who escaped into the Cumberland Mountains, even as others hid in swamps and established communities in the less traveled places in forgotten corners of their former lands.

It is out of that background of hardscrabble survival and its subsequent resurgence that current Piqua Shawnee people live and work to preserve their unique heritage. The tribe consists of several family groups that are interrelated and today have members that live in several states, and also have relatives who reside as far as in Canada. Currently the majority of Piqua's live in Alabama, with members who also live in Tennessee, Kentucky, Ohio, Indiana, Missouri, Texas, Maryland, and South Carolina. Because we are so widely dispersed, we have at least four tribal gatherings per year in alternating geographic locations, thereby preventing any of our people from having to travel much farther than the others.

Governmentally, The Piqua Shawnee have a Principal Chief, as well as a Second Chief, with the tribal government being maintained by a Tribal Council composed of clan mothers and clan chiefs, including an advisory body known as the Council of

Elders. The Tribal Council is led in accordance with Piqua Shawnee tribal traditions in mind, guided by Clan protocol; all issues are debated in council and subsequently put before the tribe's several clans for consideration and deliberation before a final decision is rendered. Piqua Shawnee tradition dictates that the function of their Tribal Council is to debate and seek consensus on all tribal matters, to facilitate the goal that the Piqua people speak with one voice. The tribal government also has modern positions, including a treasurer and secretary, which are determined by elections by the people, and for a set period of time. These elected positions do not have a vote status on the Tribal Council.

The states in which the Piqua Shawnee now reside in have in some cases chosen to acknowledge their presence and contributions to the larger society, as in 1991 when the Governor of the Commonwealth of Kentucky recognized the Piqua Sept of Ohio Shawnee as an Indian tribe. This recognition was followed by Alabama when on July 10, 2001 the Alabama Indian Affairs Commission, acting under the authority of the Davis-Strong Act recognized the Piqua Sept of Ohio Shawnee Tribe as an Indian tribe of the Yellowhammer state. This was an important event, as it made the Piqua Sept the first petitioning group to be recognized in 17 years. While today tribal enrollment will be considered by the Piqua Shawnee Tribal Council for applicants seeking enrollment who can document their Shawnee ancestry, those applicants who are "of American Indian descent other than Shawnee must provide documentation of descent from a tribe that was known to live with the Shawnee prior to the 1832 removal act".

Contact Information

Piqua Shawnee Tribe Gary Hunt, Chief
3412 Wellford Circle
Birmingham, AL 35226
E-Mail: okema@Live.com
www.piquashawnee.com

UNITED CHEROKEE ANI-YUN-WIYA NATION

The United Cherokee Ani-Yun-Wiya Nation is another of the Cherokee groups that are recognized by the state, and one that has a Tribal Council and several officers, including Principal Chief Gina Williamson, Vice Chief Lowrey Hesse, Tribal Secretary Judy Dixon, and Tribal Treasurer Donna Bridges. The tribe is headquartered at 1531 Blount Ave in Guntersville, AL.

The United Cherokee are active in preserving the heritage of the state's Native American history. Recent controversy has led to the voice of the Cherokee community being raised in defense of the ancestors of the tribe. Lowrey Hesse, the Vice Principal Chief of the United Cherokee Ani Yun Wiya Nation, gave a news conference outside of Grissom High School in Huntsville, Alabama on February 5, 2013 regarding issues concerning his people's views on an important issue. Newspaper headlines from the evening heralded that "Alabama Tribe Opposes School Relocation", as tribal members and supporters organized over issues of identity and heritage related to a proposed possible relocation of a school. These events had the United Cherokee Ani Yun Wiya Nation worried about the relocation site of the institution.

The school in question was Grissom High School in Huntsville, Alabama. The facility was located on Baily Cove Road and the proposal by administrators to possibly rebuild it on a 60-acre site, located just off of Weatherly Road raised alarms for the tribal community.

> *"We know that there are human remains there. My ancestors," Lowrey Hesse, the tribe's vice principal chief, said February 5 during a news conference, reported AL.com. "The old adage goes, 'Do you want your own grandmother dug up?' That's the way we feel, except we're a little closer to the issue than most average Americans."*

The site is one that was important not just to the Cherokee group but was to others as well; they were not the only group hoping to protect the important site. Its past was one that

concerned other citizens of Alabama as well, and when the
Tennessee Valley Archaeological Research conducted an
archaeological survey results, conducted on behalf of the Byrd
Springs Rod and Gun Club in January, the research group's
director said there are at least five archaeological sites that would
be affected if the Weatherly Road site was developed, according
to AL.com. The importance to the site as a part of the Native
American history of Alabama was keenly felt by many people and
the tribe acted to bring attention to the situation.

> *"(TVAR) recommends that all the sites within the proposed
> development be evaluated by a qualified archaeologist in
> regard to site preservation and (National Register of
> Historic Places) status prior to any further disturbances,"
> Mr. Johnson, the primary researcher behind the study
> wrote in the report. "Otherwise, a historic resource
> potentially significant to improving our understanding of
> American history and prehistory could be irretrievably lost
> during the course of construction activities on the site."*

The United Cherokee Ani-Yun-Wiya Nation handed out
relevant information at the news conference including a January
11 letter from Alabama state archaeologist Stacye Hathorn
written to Huntsville Superintendent Casey Wardynski that
detailed that there were three Native American sites on the
Weatherly Road land that contain human remains. The state of
Alabama does has a law against disturbing any human remains, a

legislation known as the Alabama Burial Act, which was signed in 2010 and would charge anyone guilty of disturbing remains with a misdemeanor. The tribe hoped such attention focused on the situation would prevent the remains of their ancestors being disturbed. According to AL.com, spokesman for the school district said research into the Weatherly Road site was still ongoing[10].

The tribe is also active in the community educating others about the values of the tribe and Native Americans in general. The simple message brought to Team Redstone employees by Gina Williams, the principal chief for the United Cherokee Ani-Yun-Wiya Nation during the National American Indian Heritage Month observance at the Sparkman Center's Bob Jones Auditorium on Nov. 24, 2015. Chief Williamson has served the United Cherokee Ani-Yun-Wiya Nation as a leader since 1998.

During the event she was joined on stage by several Ani-Yun-Wiya tribal members from the Powwow Group and Thunder Heart Drummers shared their culture through dance, song and words. The group sang "Amazing Grace" in their Cherokee language and involved several audience members in demonstrating the Snake Dance, performed on flute and drum,

---

[10] http://indiancountrytodaymedianetwork.com/2013/02/08/alabama-tribe-opposes-school-relocation-147544

and the group provided several interesting artifact displays slated at teaching Cherokee culture and its uniqueness.

> *"The way to enrich their leadership ways is by really listening to them. Listening to them is an art now. We don't really listen. We don't look in each other's face. We don't acknowledge each other," she said "We to stop what we are doing and listen. That's our future talking. They are talking right now and what they're saying is important."*

Williamson went on to say that the hope of our future is in our children, a statement of insight and rooted in Cherokee values.

> *"We've got to make the world a better place. The only way we're going to do that, I think, is through our children," she said. "We need to help fulfill the prayers of our children."*

The future for the United Cherokee Ani-Yun-Wiya Nation is secure after years of struggle to re-establish themselves as one among the many tribal governments of the state of Alabama.

Contact Information

United Cherokee Ani-Yun-Wiya Nation
1531 Blount Ave or P.O. Box 754
Guntersville, AL 35976
 (256) 582-2333
 E-Mail: to ucanonline@bellsouth.net
www.ucan-online.org or www.air-corp.org

Chief Naiche, youngest son of Cochise, Chiricahua Apache Naiche at
Mount Vernon Barracks in Alabama, 1889, photo by Reed & Wallace.

NON-STATE RECOGNIZED GROUPS

There are several communities of Native Americans which were extant during the early part of the 1900's but which faded with modernity. One is the Wildfork Indian Community in Escambia County, now mostly depopulated and marked by the Wildfork Indian Cemetery. Today there are many individuals and families which have roots in this once thriving settlement of Indian people that is now dispersed. Glenn Simmons and other descendants of this community carry on the heritage of Native American culture and identity that was hard fought in the days of Jim Crow segregation that overshadowed Wildfork in generations past. As Glenn Simmons puts it in his popular blog about Native American spirituality, the ties that bind Individual, Community, and Spirituality run deep.

> *"Those that dare to step into the dance of the unknown, to trust the Creator have never said they have all the answers. In reality the deeper they step into the unknown it's understood that answers aren't the interesting part. Answers are no longer the desire. Reality and connection, then relationship come from the journey, the ebb and flow, the tides of the spiral."*

Chavers Indian School that the family of Glenn Simmons attended in Wildfork, Alabama. Courtesy of the "Brewton Historical Society"

WILDFORK INDIAN COMMUNITY OF ESCAMBIA COUNTY, ALABAMA

There are many places where once communities of mixed blood people lived but who faded into the general population or other tribes once the rigid social order of the past ended. Some of the old Indian settlements that had survived the removal and existed during the Jim Crow era faded with the twentieth century, the people of these settlements going their own way in many cases, making lives outside the tribal settlement. Across the south were dozens of pockets of Indian people, many descendants of the migrations of Eastern Siouan groups out of the Carolinas and Virginia which had been happening since Colonial times. Many families would intermarry among themselves and the taint of their "mixed" origins often times meant they were marginalized in the places they settled, living in small family clusters and avoiding interactions with outsiders.

In southern Alabama not far from the much larger community of Eastern Creeks in the area of Atmore was the Wildfork community. Though the Creeks who lived across Escambia, Monroe, and Baldwin Counties of Alabama were much more well known to outsiders due to their greater numbers, and to a smaller degree the fame of some of the Creek leaders and warriors whose names were famous in state history that they descended from, the less well known Eastern Siouan descendants of Wildfork settlement too faced the same difficult struggle for identity that the Creeks did. Wildfork was a small and insular community, dominated by the Evans, Chavers, Kennedy, Williams, and other families of Known Indian ancestry.

Initially settled by migrating Indian mixed blood families from the Carolinas in the early 1800s on the heels of the removal of the larger Indian nations, it would prosper for a century before declining to the sleepy hamlet it is today, and like many others it would decline with the span of the century as a distinct community. Like other small tribal settlements across the region, during the 1800's some of its descendants would continue in the turning wheel of intermarriage among the group and into others such groups, while some would marry out into the local white population. Wildfork was just one of many dozens mixed race groups across the eastern US which were caught in between the races of the binary White, Black racial categorization used legally across the south, an elsewhere.

A 1953 article by Edward Price called "Geographical Analysis of White-Negro-Indian Racial Mixtures in the Eastern United States by Edward T. Price, Los Angeles State College, though dated does give insights to the Chavers family. The following excerpt is from the Association of American Geographers Annals Vol. 43 (June 1953) pp 138-55.

> "Another widespread name among mixed-bloods is Chavis (Chavous, Chavers, probably Shavers, etc.) Whereas Goins was more frequent among free colored people than whites, Chavis was also more numerous among the free colored. One free Negro of the name rose to fame as an educator. Chavis is a prominent Croatan name. It has been reported in South Carolina as a mixed-blood name, e.g., In Orangeburg County, and its association with the

Melungeons and Redbones is suggested by the records. A Granville County muster roll of 1754 lists three members of the family, one as a Negro, the other two (at least one a son of the first) as mulattoes. Colored slaveholders of the name were identified in Virginia by Jackson in Charlotte County and Russell in Mecklenburg County. They are identified as South Carolina frontiersmen in 1751 and 1752. Again an interesting story should unfold could the family and name be traced to their beginnings."

As the article suggests, much research has gone into digging up the origins and journeys of many of the mixed blood families, most of whose surnames are repeatedly found through the many communities of mixed race people. In this sleepy corner of Alabama, individuals from the Chavers, Evans, Williams, and Kennedy families struggled to survive the poverty and bigotry that were daily challenges. Wildfork was a poor and isolated places, where only family could be depended on. Though today the Wildfork of those bygone days has disappeared, the lives of its people give us insight into the times.

An example of such an individual from this community was Andrew Jackson Chavers. Born the son of William B. Chavers and his wife, Esther Williams, on November 3, 1844 in Greenville, Conecuh, Alabama, he grew to adulthood during one of the darkest periods in Southeastern Indian history. Only a few years before the forcible round up of many Creeks had occurred and the handful of Indians who remained behind were careful in their dealings with strangers. Unlike some of his kinsmen who would stay to weather lives of discrimination and poverty in the southern Alabama hardscrabble struggle, he would leave Alabama and journey to a new life in Texas, just as countless other families of Eastern Siouan origin had been doing for over a century even then.

Large communities of interrelated families had been established in the west and a steady flow of new migrants sustained these often independent and isolated settlements in Texas, Louisiana and other areas. Rough and ready for action, the lives of those who did go west often times had violent endings. According to family Lore, "Jack" Chavers was last seen at the local saloon playing cards on the night he would disappear. The tradition in the Chavers family is that three Negro traders drowned him in the Brazos River about 1905 after an altercation. He does appear on the 1900 Texas census and no records exist for him after this time, and the family lore is most likely correct. The frontier was a bloody place at times. Elizabeth Gaffard was the wife of Andrew Jackson Chavers, and accompanied him in the family journey west to Texas. She was the daughter of Albert Gafford. She and "Jack" Chavers were wed on February 27, 1866 in Butler County, Alabama. She died on April 3, 1912 at the home of her daughter, Dora Williams and is buried at the Salem Cemetery, Freestone County, Texas.

Like Chavers, Kennedy is a well-documented name among many of the Carolina diaspora groups of mixed bloods, and was prominent among the Wildfork people too. The Kennedy family like the Chavers and several others came to south Alabama together. Richard Kennedy was born about 1800 in North Carolina. His wife Elizabeth Chavers, the daughter of John "Chavous" was born about 1803 in South Carolina and passed on about 1880. Like so many migrating groups of eastern Siouan origins, the family would relocate to Henry County, Alabama. The Kennedy according to some were like the Chavers and others of Wildfork, at times counted among the Creek Indians, though they were of Carolina Eastern Siouan origins. They ran a school for Indians in Wildfork; It gave the children a place to get an education outside of the system of white or colored schools the counties mandated, with the school at Wildfork still being open as late as the 1930's.

The children born of Richard and Elizabeth Chavers Kennedy were several. Dempsey Kennedy born 1834; married in July of 1853 in Henry Co., Ala. to Nancy Whitehead. Both are buried at Pleasant Hill Church Cemetery, which is also called the Old Wildfork Indian Cemetery. Annie Kennedy was born in 1833;

married on July 23, 1860 in Henry Co., Ala. to William Smith. Elizabeth Kennedy was born December 16, of 1831 and passed on January 14, 1886. She married on November 28, 1853 in Henry Co., Ala. to Henry Whitehead. Henry Kennedy was born August 9, of 1835 and passed away May 30, 1907 in Brewton, in Escambia County, Alabama. He married a Susan whose identity is unknown as yet, she being born Jan 15, 1848 and passing on July 16, 1907. Baberris Kennedy was born 1835. He was wed on November 20, 1856 in Henry Co., Ala. to a Mahala Mills. Richard and Elizabeth's children would also include Richard Alabam Kennedy (born 1836), Christian Berry Kennedy (born 1841), Calvin Kennedy (born in 1843 and married on February 23, 1862 in Henry Co., Ala. to Hester Anderson, and Pearcy Ann Kennedy born in 1848.

The Chavers family of the Wildfork settlement was related to the Kennedy family and many times these groups of related families would relocate to a new area together with kinship being a major force in their lives; this group had come to Wildfork from the Carolinas and like many other of the Eastern Siouan groups would within a few generations continue to migrate on to Louisiana and Texas in some numbers. The Redbones and other groups in the west would grow strong over the years with the arrival of more families from the east. The migrations of some of these families during the historic era are much clearer than the initial origins which gave birth too many of them. Three quarters of a century ago, Edward Price asserted in his research on settlements like Wildfork and others their complicated beginnings.

> "The mixed-blood groups generally appear to have arisen from diverse sources. Where records are available, they indicate that the ancestors of the present mixed- bloods, coming into their present areas at the time of American settlement, were themselves mixed. The mixing must have had a beginning, of course; the old records are lacking for the easternmost groups where settlement was earlier. The surnames of the mixed-blood people are usually distinctive in their areas; if their names are taken from white people, such event seems to pre-date settlement in the present areas."

Since the research began to be compiled on these families and their settlements generations ago, the gathering of documentation regarding the source and subsequent experiences of families like the Chavers, Evans, Williams, and Kennedy families has continued. Sometimes oral histories carried by descendants are helpful, along with colonial, state, tribal, and federal records, to reveal the truly complex identity of such communities. One of the historians of the PeeDee people of South Carolina, Michelle Schohn, is quoted as stating of the her Chavers family that they

"Came from the Pee Dee River... In the early 1700's, we worked closely with the colonial government. Many of us moved to the Goose Creek area to work with the government as traders. In 1738, they established a reservation for us on land formerly owned by James Coachman on the Edisto River. After a short time, we moved upriver to the Goodland Swamp area of Orangeburg County to establish a better trading position. Then along came the Revolutionary War and James' nephew, James Coachman, together with Captain John Allston established a company of 50 Pee Dee Indians called the Raccoon Company or the Foot Rangers. After one year, that company was absorbed into Col William Thompson's Third Regiment. Col. Thompson also came from Orangeburg County and was familiar with us, which is likely part of the reason our company was merged with his regiment. Fortunately for us, that regiment had a muster roll, so we have the list of those soldiers' names. Most of us descend from someone on that list." [11]

One of the foremost scholars of the mixed blood groups in the Eastern United States, Calvin Beal, had written in 1971 locating the Chavers family with

"A sizeable Creek remnant in Alabama centered in Escambia County...the Creek chief Calvin McGhee claimed that in the 19th century a Creek named Richard Kennedy married a local Chavers girl, named Elizabeth. Kennedy

---

[11] from an E-mail to Pamela Call Johnson, April 9, 1999

also had children by Elizabeth's sister and they retained
the name of Chavers. The Kennedy and Chavers
descendants had an elementary school of their own in the
locality called Wild Fork near Breton. One elderly woman
of the group told the chief that they were from the
Carolinas and were Catawba."

There was indeed an 1880 Escambia County Alabama census which lists an Indian Kennedy family, and in which the 80 year old mother, listed as the head of the household and named Elizabeth, is enumerated as born in South Carolina. Like some of the Wildfork people's ancestors, many of the male founders of some of the common surnames of the Poarch Creeks near them were Eastern Siouan migrants, especially Catawba and Lumbee, with families such as Dees, Gibson, Hosford, and others coming from such men. Florence Bush, a researcher in this area as well claims asserts her Chavers great-great grandmother was from the Catawba people originally. Bush posits that she came from Rutherford County, in North Carolina and goes on to state the Chavers, (as Catawba)

"Were once one of the most powerful Siouan tribes in
North America. They originally lived in Tennessee and
North Carolina. They were active on the colonist side
during the Revolution. As a result, they were given land in
York and Lancaster Counties in South Carolina. The

estimate for full-blooded Catawba still living is about 350. They were noted for their pottery and basketry."

The quandary many families like the Kennedy and Chavers of Wildfork confronted over suspicions of their white neighbors as to their racial identity was common and rooted in the social realities of the time.

> *"Throughout most of American history, the legal, social, educational, and economic disadvantages of being African-American were so great that it was better to be almost anything else. It is also good to keep in mind that American law did not differentiate between the status of tri-racial, mulatto, and Negro. Some records list as mulatto anyone who seemed to them to appear physically non-white meaning Asian, Spanish, and so forth. Also, on one census a person might be recorded as mulatto or Black and on another as White and it would be the same person"*

Virginia E. DeMarce, a respected academic and researcher on Eastern Indians explains. DeMarce forwards that these families were indeed facing difficult lives due to perceptions of them as of questionable origins. They were relegated to the edge of the social order of the times, dwelling on unwanted lands and out of the way refuges.

> *"The major mid-1700 concentrations of the family were in south-central Virginia and north-central North Carolina and later subdivided into Orange, Person, and Caswell*

counties. Many of these families lived in places that were economically marginal – swamps, marshes, hills and hollows. Several family names appear over and over again with great persistence namely Bass, Chavers, and Goins. One of the most common tri-racial family names, Chavis [Chavers] and its variants, is a clear source of African American heritage."

Some research find ties to Melungeon families of the Tennessee area as well as other groups as well. Indeed recent research conducted among the mixed blood groups using new genetic research and other untapped areas of inquiry lend credence to complex ties among all the groups. Information on the Chavers family showing they might be connected to the Appalachian Melungeons is frequent and the family has many lines of evidence linking the families of Wildfork to them and other of the Eastern Siouan diaspora populations. There are without doubt deep connections between the Chavers, Kennedy and other families at Wildfork and the Melungeon people of the Appalachian Mountains to the north.

The Melungeon name refers to a specific set of families living in the Mountains. Often dark-featured and usually visibly different from their non-Melungeon neighbors, they have lived in southwest Virginia and northeast Tennessee for centuries according to the documentary records. The specific origin of the

Melungeons, like the Wildfork people has been a source of debate for nearly as long. Though some of the Melungeon's themselves claim that their ancestors are Portuguese, others Native American, and others gypsy, Turkish, or Jewish, the roots of the group was for many generations a complete mystery.

The ambiguity of their identity made whites suspicious. The local whites would oft time isolate the Melungeon's to their own small communities. Through the years, in places like Newman's Ridge and the Blackwater Valley of Tennessee the families of these settlements evolved a distinct and lasting identity. As the Melungeon Heritage Association observed, like the people of Wildfork, their kinsmen in the mountain had challenges to their place in the social order of the day constantly.

> *"In nearly a dozen court cases, the ethnicity of Melungeon people was challenged, including one case in which several members of the group were tried for illegal voting. They were accused on the grounds that they were not white and therefore ineligible to cast a ballot. While they were acquitted, this kind of legal discrimination, along with a general social stigma, dogged the Melungeons well into the twentieth century."*

As Price observed in his 1953 article, the ties amongst the Wildfork people and not unlike so many of the other isolated groups like them, is difficult to pin down precisely; especially the early origins and subsequent interconnections with related groups.

> *"Though certain facts concerning the origin of these peoples have been traced, the questions of who they were and why they displayed this unusual clannishness have hardly been touched. The relationships mentioned suggest the hypothesis of a colonial mixed-blood society having origin in Virginia and the Carolinas, consisting of a number of localized concentrations as well as floaters who served to maintain or affect both blood and social ties between the sedentary groups. Though the early groups certainly grew by accretion, chance colonization of a few members of this society in a new location may have been the necessary condition for a new localization of the same type. They seem to have moved westward into and across the Appalachians with the general stream of population. It is difficult to trace specific parenthood of one group by another, but numerous interrelationships are indicated by the records."*

Today little remains of the Old Wildfork settlement besides a cemetery and a few families still in the area, though a few of the families once part of that community now are involved with state recognized tribes, as well as the larger Native American community in other areas. Intermarriage with local whites and the isolation of the area even yet has led to many of the descendants of the very community knowing little of its ties to other Indian groups or the history of struggle and survival that a community such as Wildfork exemplified. The graves of the people of the community may be the most lasting testament to their place in the struggle of Indian people to remain in the south and define their own destinies.

A 1999 review of the Pleasant Hill Church Cemetery, historically known as the Old Wildfork Indian Cemetery, shows the surnames of many of the families which are present in the majority of the mixed race settlements (formerly called tri-racial isolates) across the eastern US. Families like Kennedy, Chavers, and Evans are among the people of a past generation now buried in the Old Wild Fork Indian Cemetery.

These are some of the groups which have made some contact with authorities but whom have not received federal nor state recognition, and may have been or be in the process of petitioning for recognition, and their last known status per BIA OFA[12].

- ❖ Cherokee Nation of Alabama (Letter of Intent to Petition 02/16/1999)
- ❖ Cherokee River Indian Community (Letter of Intent to Petition 08/03/2000, Receipt of Petition 08/03/2000),

---

[12] Recent changes to the BIA Office of federal Acknowledgement regulations have dropped tribes which did not have submitted petitions on file, and many tribes who were out of contact or lacking documentation beyond a letter of intent to petition are now removed from the list of petitioners.

Non-State Recognized Groups

- ❖ Chickamauga Cherokee of Alabama
- ❖ Chickmaka Band of the South Cumberland Plateau
- ❖ Coweta Creek Tribe (Letter of Intent to Petition 2/12/2003)
- ❖ Eagle Bear Band of Free Cherokees
- ❖ The Langley Band of the Chickamogee Cherokee Indians of the Southeastern United States, aka Langley Band of Chickamogee of Cherokee Indians)(Letter of Intent to Petition 04/20/1994, Postal service certified letter returned 11/5/1997)
- ❖ Phoenician Cherokee II - Eagle Tribe of Sequoyah (Letter of Intent to Petition 09/18/2001)
- ❖ Principal Creek Indian Nation East of the Mississippi (Letter of Intent to Petition 11/09/1971 Declined to Acknowledge 06/10/1985, certified letter returned "not known" 10/1997), Wolf Creek Cherokee Tribe, Inc. of Florida

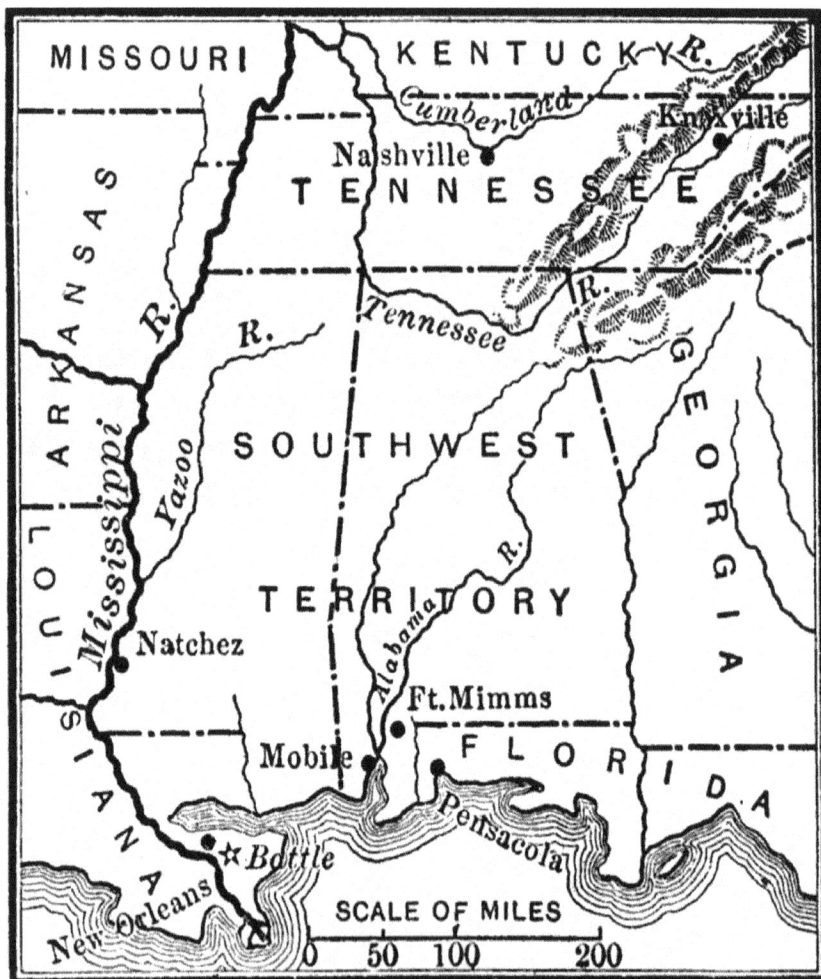

Map Territorial with Modern State Overlay

EPILOGUE

The tribes of Alabama are flourishing today. They are moving forward with efforts at preserving their languages, cultures, and heritage even as they seek new opportunities for economic development, infrastructure improvement, housing and other goals very present and modern. The heritage of the state is deeply tied to these communities and the relationship between the two groups is one that after years of difficulty is today improving and beneficial to all.

Today's Native American

Modern social statistics of American Indian people in the United States allow for the defining of particular characteristics of contemporary Native American life, including Native Americans in Alabama. These numbers can be compared to the average citizens' social statistics to gain important insights into the forces shaping modern Indian lives and communities. There are many areas that such revealing data can be insightful, including current demographic trends, economic development, and health care standards. Important issues such as drug and alcohol abuse, domestic violence, tribal economic development and other such data can facilitate a better understanding of contemporary Native American life. That the health care provided for American Indian populations have glaring disparities from those of other American racial and ethnic populations is well documented, despite the efforts of the IHS.

The likelihood of a Native American to have higher rates of many diseases, significantly higher rates of premature death, and inadequate medical coverage is long established and little changed from the past; traditions of unhealthy food and lifestyles which the south has long lived with continue to affect Indians negatively. Issues that are unduly impacting the Native Americans such as methamphetamine and alcohol abuse on many large reservations are a challenge being faced by both tribal and federal governments by a few tribes of the state who are reservated such as Poarch Band of Creeks and MOWA Choctaws. The loss of tribal land base is another looming challenge facing many tribes in Indian Country, even as many Alabama tribes still have no commonly held tribal lands. While Native Americans lost more than 97.7 percent of the pre-contact land once held by tribal nations over the course of the American conquest, a few are seeing success in efforts to recover viable land bases, such as Poarch Band and the MOWA Choctaw.

Epilouge

Identification of Native Americans

The Native American identity in the United States is a
complex matter, and not given to simple definitions which can
encompass the whole of the many aspects of identity any person
or peoples have. It is doubtless that the ongoing dialogue and
struggles to define the essence of "Native American" or
"American Indian" identity both for people who see themselves
as Native Americans and for those who don't. While there are a
number of different terminologies about Native identity which
have been used to define "Indianness" in the past, the origin and
the potential use of the definition can play a part in what
definition is most accurate. "Indianness" can include culture,
society, genetics, biology, law, and self-identification, all being
just some of the influences which create the meaning of this term
in particular contexts. In the south especially where 20 percent of
the "white" population has recent African ancestry according to
new studies in genetics, these "hidden ancestors" are often
perceived as being Indian in oral histories, as this was a safer
identity in times past.

Important to these contexts is how many American
Indians adapt and adjust to the dominant American society, an
experience which may be called an "oppositional process" and
one in which the boundaries between Native Americans and the

dominant social groups are defined. "Ethnogenesis", a process by which the ethnic identity of the group is developed and renewed as social organizations and cultures evolve, is one way to describe the Native American experience in America over time; indeed, the question of personal and social identity, especially aboriginal identity, is one that is somewhat common in countless societies globally. Indians in Alabama like people everywhere are facing greater challenges to answering the age old question; who am I?

Today the ways that Indianness is defined in the United States are diverse. Traditional definitions of "Indian-ness" are still important to many, and that there is a sense of "tribal" identity connecting Indianness to sacred traditions, familiar places, and a shared common history as an indigenous people should be expected. Language is also viewed to be an important part of identity, and retention of Native American languages, especially for young people in a community, is an important part in a tribe's survival.

For many members of federally recognized tribal groups, such as the Poarch Band of Creeks, a common source of a definition for 'being Indian' is their CDIB blood quantum, which for the Poarch Band like many other tribes, is often a one-quarter blood Native American ancestry threshold for eligibility for enrollment. In state recognized and other tribes it is some type of documented Indian heritage which is needed to enroll. The utilization of the blood quantum is being questioned as a viable method, especially as Indians marry out to other ethnic groups at a higher rate than any other United States ethnic or racial category, and in the eyes of some could ultimately lead to their racial assimilation into the rest of an increasingly multiracial American social fabric of the 21st century.

The federal census data indeed provides important insights to the quality of life in many tribal communities, federal, state, urban, and unrecognized. The Indian population has seen exponential growth during the 20th century. According to 2008 US Census projections, those who were enumerated as being Native American and Alaska Natives solely are numbered a bit more than 3 million, admittedly a small sliver of the total US population of 304 million. This statistic means that Native American people are about 1 percent of the entire population of the United States. Persons who identified as Native American alone or who were enumerated as inclusive with other racial groups are identified as about 4.86 million individuals, or 1.60 percent of America's total population. The population in the U.S. of Native Americans continues to grow annually at a healthy rate, and projections that American Indian and Alaska Natives will reach 5 million by 2065 have been forwarded by the Census

Bureau. Today the relationship between the federal government and an Indian tribe is important to their access to resources, and currently 566 federally recognized tribes are acknowledged by the American government through the trust relationship they share.

The amount of people who identify as being Native Americans extends well beyond the aforementioned tribal entities with federal recognition, or even state recognition as with the many tribes we have looked at in this work. The United States of American hosts 2.4 million self-identified "Native Americans", and many of these American Indians have for much of the years past lived in extreme poverty, both on and off of reservations, though the larger western reservations have felt the brunt of the inability of federal policy to address important issues facing these populations. Even the two comparatively small tribes of Alabama who do have reservations, the MOWA Choctaw and the Poarch Band of Creeks face real challenges.

Poverty

Many Indian communities remain poor, regardless of size or status. To some degree Indian gaming enterprises have assisted some tribal communities make inroads to the problem of poverty such as recent successes by the Poarch Band of Creeks , yet the majority of Native Americans still face economic hardship, especially the more remote reservations and numbers of urban Indian poor. The suite of difficulties that families find comes along with poverty such as substance abuse, joblessness and homelessness, diminished opportunities, crime, and others continue to challenge even the most vigorous efforts at their eradication. The struggle continues for many tribes.

Indeed some Indian governing bodies have to some degree taken more control of their economies and have begun to improve the quality of life for their members, reservations especially face unique challenges, and where bridging the many gaps created by the Native American experience is still a major issue. While the federal Census data from both 1990 and 2000 show that poverty is still a major issue on many reservations and that Native Americans have the highest rates of poverty and unemployment, the poverty rate of many Native American communities, now at 25%, is indeed a call to actions for social reform in the eyes of many. With a median income of Native American households of $19,900, the challenge of overcoming the lack of jobs in many tribal communities leads many tribes to seek new avenues of economic development. Indeed, Indian tribes are becoming increasingly economically independent of the programs once hallmarks of the economic landscapes of tribal life.

According to the Census Bureau, real per capita income has grown substantially in past decade, and even while economic conditions on many Indian reservations has improved, it is overall still significantly less than that of the their fellow United States citizens. Recent poverty rates from statistics show that Native Americans are among the highest among any race; Reservation Indians have a 39% poverty rate while Non-Reservation Indians are at 26%. African Americans show 25%, Hispanic of all races, 23%, Pacific Islander, 18%, Asian, 13%; and Whites show 9%. These statistics reveal the challenges many Indians in Alabama face.

Health

Indian people also face a disproportional share of those with certain diseases. While disease and epidemics are commonly thought of as being endemic to native communities, such as alcoholism rife on some tribal lands and surrounding areas, there are also any other diseases, such as diabetes, that have a prominent presence among Indian people. The federal census data shows that out of the 'single race' population of Native Americans and Native Alaskans, around 16.8% of individuals have a disability of some kind. Native Americans have the highest rate of smoking among all races and ethnic groups, about 32.2% of Native American adults as of 2008 were smokers, in contrast to a rate of 21.8% for white adults. In areas such as alcoholism, illicit drug use,

All Native Americans today live within the larger American culture, to lesser of greater degrees. The mainstream American culture is one that dominates not only Indian tribal cultures but is impacting cultures around the globe. The social isolation many Indians in Alabama face does not insulate them from the impacts of these events. One way to define culture is a set of values and practices that are shared by the members of a group, values that can be expressed many ways and are often reinforced through art, stories, songs, rituals, and language. All of these are crucial to the preservation of any culture, especially those which have histories of attempts to wipe them out as do those of most tribes who remain in Alabama.

The Indian people still in Alabama are the survivors of a great many who were not able to withstand the journey of the last 500 years. The Native American culture has always been the beating heart of Indian identity. History shows us that colonial authorities and later the American government created policies that sought to control and suppress Native American tribal cultures, beginning from first contact and extending into the 20th century. Indians were to be assimilated into the dominate European "civilization", yet somehow these communities survived. It's without doubt that much has been lost, and every community lost some, if not much, of their original culture in the years since first contact with Europeans. For countless communities of Native Americans who once lived in Alabama, all that remains of their time on the land is a place name, a story of a lost time or place, or a tree covered mound in a farmer's field.

Looking Ahead

The present success of many tribes in Alabama says unequivocally that some communities did retain their most important cultural expressions of identity, and those are seeing a rebirth in interest of their arts, stories and rituals. In fact, some tribes are tired of non-Indian "wannabes" trying to adopt parts of Native American culture without any real ancestry and without being willing to take on the responsibilities that tribal membership brings with it, and such concerns are inspiring new approached to defining Native American identity both internally and externally. Language, culture, and tribal identity are emerging more as concerns rather than just being "recognized as Indians" as in the past. A more nuanced posture is being observed among the leadership of some tribes as a new generation of leaders arrives to put their own stamp on the identity of their community and state.

ALABAMA COMMISSION OF INDIAN AFFAIRS COMMISSIONERS

- ❖ Ma-Chis Lower Creek; Nancy Carnley (1) 64 Private Road 1312 Elba, AL 36323 (334) 897-3207 E-Mail: machis@centurytel.net
- ❖ Poarch Band of Creeks; Eddie Tullis 188 Lynn McGhee Drive Atmore, AL 36502 (251) 368-2685 E-Mail: eddietullis@yahoo.com

- ❖ Echota Cherokees; Stanley Trimm 410 Main Street West Glencoe, AL 35904 (256) 492-8678 E-Mail: stanleyandhelen@bellsouth.net
- ❖ Cherokee Tribe of Northeast; Alabama Stan Long 113 Parker Drive Huntsville, AL 35811 (256) 426-6344 E-Mail: stan.long11@gmail.com
- ❖ United Cherokee Ani-Yun-Wiya Nation; Lowrey Hesse 1531 Blount Ave or P.O. Box 754 Guntersville, AL 35976 (256) 582-2333 E-Mail: to ucanonline@bellsouth.net or www.ucan-online.org or www.air-corp.org
- ❖ Cher-O-Creek Intra Tribal Indians; Violet P. Hamilton 1315 Northfield Circle Dothan, AL 36303 (334) 596-4866 E-Mail: vlt_hamilton@yahoo.com
- ❖ Commission's Appointee; Vacant
- ❖ Southeastern Mvskoke Nation; Martha C. Williams P.O. Box 296 Midland City, AL 36350 (334) 983-3723 E-Mail: mcwilliams@sw.rr.com
- ❖ Speaker of House's Appointee; Representative Harry Shiver Alabama State House 11 South Union Street, Suite 526-D Montgomery, AL 36130 (334) 242-7745 E-Mail: harryshiver@aol.com
- ❖ Lieutenant Governor's Appointee; Senator Tom Whatley, Alabama State House 11 South Union Street, Room 733 Montgomery, AL 36130 (334) 242-7865 E-Mail: tom.whatley@alsenate.gov
- ❖ MOWA Band Of Choctaws; Lebaron Byrd 1080 Red Fox Road Mount Vernon, AL 36560 (251) 829-5500 E-Mail: lebaronbyrd@aol.com

- ❖ Piqua Shawnee Tribe; Don Rankin 3412 Wellford Circle Birmingham, AL 35226-2616 (205) 979-6581 E-Mail: kahkahwee@charter.net
- ❖ Governor's Appointee; Robert E. Brasher 101 Fords Valley Road Fayette, AL 35555-6975 (205) 442-3535 E-Mail: cherokeebob@earthlink.net

(1) BOARD CHAIRPERSON (2) BOARD VICE-CHAIRPERSON

CONTACT INFORMATION FOR TRIBES

- ❖ Alabama Indian Affairs Commission; 771 South Lawrence Street, Suite 106 Montgomery, AL 36130 (334) 240-0998 Fax: (334) 240-3408 E-Mail: aiac@att.net
- ❖ Poarch Band of Creek Indians; 5811 Jack Springs Road Atmore, AL 36502 (251) 368-9136 www.poarchcreekindians.org
- ❖ Echota Cherokee Tribe of Alabama; Tribal Leaders Stanley Trimm, Charlotte Hallmark 410 Main Street West, Glencoe, AL 35904 (256) 492-8678 E-Mail: stanleyandhelen@bellsouth.net www.echotacherokeetribe.homestead.com
- ❖ Cherokee Tribe of Northeast Alabama, Stan Long, Chief; 113 Parker Drive Huntsville, AL 35811 (256) 426-6344 E-Mail: stan.long11@gmail.com www.cherokeetribeofnortheastalabama.com

- ❖ MaChis Lower Creek Indian Tribe of Alabama; 202 North Main Street Kinston, Alabama 36453 (334)565-3207 Email: machis@centurytel.net
- ❖ Southeastern Mvskoke Nation; Ronnie F. Williams, Chief; P.O. Box 296, Midland City, AL 36350 (334) 983-3723
- ❖ Cher-O-Creek Intra Tribal Indians; Violet Parker Hamilton, Chief Po Box 717, Dothan, AL 36303 1315 Northfield Circle, Dothan, AL 36303 (334) 596-4866 E-Mail: vlt_hamilton@yahoo.com
- ❖ MOWA Band of Choctaw Indians; Chief Framon Weaver 1080 Red Fox Road Mount Vernon, AL 36560 (251) 829-5500 E-Mail: lebaronbyrd@aol.com www.mowa-choctaw.com
- ❖ Piqua Shawnee; Tribe Gary Hunt, Chief 3412 Wellford Circle Birmingham, AL 35226 E-Mail: okema@Live.com www.piquashawnee.com
- ❖ United Cherokee Ani-Yun-Wiya Nation; 1531 Blount Ave or P.O. Box 754 Guntersville, AL 35976 (256) 582-2333 E-Mail: to ucanonline@bellsouth.net www.ucan-online.org or www.air-corp.org.

RESEARCH RESOURCES

CHEROKEE

- ❖ A list is available of the Cherokees living in Alabama in 1851: Siler, David W. The Eastern Cherokees, A Census of the Cherokee Nation in North Carolina, Tennessee, Alabama and Georgia in 1851. Cottonport, Louisiana: Polyanthus, 1972. FHL book 970.3 C424sd. This list contains the names of each person's father, mother and children, with their ages and relationship (De Kalb, Jackson, and Marshall Counties). An index is included

- ❖ For a history of the Cherokees to about 1835, and a map showing the Cherokee towns in the Alabama area, see: Malone, Henry Thompson. Cherokees of the Old South: A People in Transition. Athens, Georgia: University of Georgia Press, 1956. FHL book 970.3 C424ma See the maps before the preface. At the end of the book there is a bibliography.

- ❖ Tyner, James W. Those Who Cried: The 16,000: A Record of the Individual Cherokees Listed in the United States Official Census of the Cherokee Nation Conducted in 1835. N.p.: Chi-ga-u, 1974. FHL book 970.3 C424tj Non-Cherokee census takers in 1835 made lists of Cherokees in Alabama, Georgia, North Carolina, and Tennessee. There are some errors because they did not understand the native languages. The government defined a person as an Indian if he or she had one-quarter degree of Indian blood. The book is indexed and has excellent maps for that period and it provides enumeration of the name of the head of the household and the number of whites and full-, half-, or quarter-blood Indians present in the household, as well as the occupations, number of slaves owned, whether the people read English or Cherokee, and in some cases if they owned a home, farm, or mill.

❖ United States. Bureau of Indian Affairs. Cherokee Agency. Records of the Cherokee Agency in Tennessee, 1801–1835. National Archives Microfilm Publications, M0208. Washington, D.C.: National Archives, 1952. FHL films 1024418–31. These records deal with the entire Cherokee Nation. They contain information about passes given to people during 1801 to 1804 allowing them to go through the Cherokee lands. These records also mention claims filed 1816 to 1833 and include the names of Army officers at posts; unauthorized settlements on Indian lands; land office records; and names of traders, settlers, missionaries, chiefs and members of the tribe. See the introduction at the beginning of the first film to learn about the contents of these records. Many individuals are listed, however there is no index.

❖ United States. Office of Indian Affairs. Letters
Received, 1824–1881; Registers of Letters
Received, 1824–1880. National Archives Microfilm
Publications, M0018, M0234. Washington, D.C.:
National Archives, 1942, 1956. FHL film 1638620
(first of 1088 films) There are letters in this
collection pertaining to each of the major tribes,
but they are not indexed.

CREEK

❖ Snider, Billie Ford. Full Name Indexes, Eastern
Creek Indians East of the Mississippi. Pensacola,
Florida: Antique Compiling, 1993. FHL fiche
6126087; book 970.3 C861sb This source lists
ancestors of the Eastern Creeks living in 1814 and
descendants to about 1972. The final chapter
contains a detailed history of the Creeks from the
1600s to 1973 and offers suggestions for Eastern
Creek Indian ancestral research.

❖ Stiggins, George. Creek Indian History: A Historical
Narrative of the Genealogy, Traditions and
Downfall of the Ispocoga or Creek Indian Tribe of
Indians. Birmingham, Alabama: Birmingham Public
Library Press, 1989. FHL book 970.3 C861s A
bibliography is found on pages 166–70.

❖ Eggleston, George Cary. Red Eagle and the Wars
with the Creek Indians. New York: Dodd, Mead and

Company Publishers, 1878. Digital version at
FamilySearch Books Online - free.

❖ Rolls were prepared in 1832 of the Lower Creeks
and the Upper Creeks. They contain the names of
principal chiefs and heads of households, where
they resided, number of people in the household
and whether they owned slaves: Abbott, Thomas J.
Creek Census of 1832 (Lower Creeks). Laguna Hills,
California: Histree, 1987. FHL book 970.3 C861a
this is indexed by name. Parsons, Benjamin S. Creek
Census of 1832 (Upper Creeks). Laguna Hills,
California: Histree, 1987. FHL book 970.3 C861pa
this is indexed by name.

SHAWNEE

❖ Shawnee!!, James Howard, Ohio University Press
❖ Tecumseh..a Life, John Sugden, Henry Holt
❖ The History of Alabama, Albert Pickett (originally
pub,1851 reprinted 1962), Birmingham Book and
Magazine
❖ The Shawnee, Jerry E. Clark, The University of
Kentucky Press
❖ Tukabatchee, Archaeological Investigations at an
historic Creek town Elmore County, Alabama 1984,
by Vernon James Knight, Jr., The University of
Alabama.

RESEARCH RESOURCES

ONLINE

- https://glennsimmons.wordpress.com/
- http://www.helphaskell.com/projectcoordinators.html
- https://www.youtube.com/watch?v=cTseLxGZZcU
- http://aiac.alabama.gov/
- www.poarchcreekindians.org
- www.echotacherokeetribe.homestead.com
- www.cherokeetribeofnortheastalabama.com
- www.machistribe.net
- www.mowa-choctaw.com
- www.piquashawnee.com
- www.ucan-online.org

GENERAL INFORMATION

- **Pickett, Albert James**. History of Alabama and Incidentally of Georgia and Mississippi, From the Earliest Period. Sheffield, Alabama: R.C. Randolph, 1896. FHL film 924406; book 976.1 H2p; a chronological history of the events affecting the Indians of the south to about 1820.
- **Young, Mary Elizabeth**. Redskins, Ruffle shirts and Rednecks: Indian Allotments in Alabama and Mississippi 1830–1860. The Civilization of the American Indian Series. Norman. Oklahoma: University of Oklahoma Press, 1961. FHL book 970.1 Y86r a work which describes the opening up

and sale of Chickasaw, Choctaw, and Creek Indian lands until about the 1840s and includes an excellent bibliography found at the end of the book.

INDEX

www.ingramcontent.com/pod-product-compliance
Lightning Source LLC
Chambersburg PA
CBHW031159270326
41931CB00006B/331